Thank you for choosing Jane Winter™

COPYRIGHT AND LICENSE

Jane Winter™ is a brand owned by Julia Art. Copyright © 2020 Julia Art. No part of this book may be reproduced without written permission from Julia Art.

By buying this book, you agree to adhere to all relevant laws in your jurisdiction and to my **License Agreement**, which can be fount at: https://jane-winter.com/license-agreement/

While I try to keep the information in this book up-to-date and correct, I provide no representations or warranties for information provided.

If you don't agree to these terms, please return the book to the store of purchase.

Do you have a question?
Please visit my website: https://jane-winter.com/ for more information and contact details.

https://jane-winter.com/license-agreement/

Jane Winter

Do you want to join our community?

FACEBOOK PAGE AND GROUP

Do you want to **share your colored pages** from my books on social media and get a lot of likes and comments?

Do you want to **get tips for coloring** and learn from our **creative community**?

Like my **FB page** and join our **Group**! You will find additional coloring pages there - you can **download them FOR FREE!**

Post your colored pages in our group! I will repost some of them on my FB page, to give you more exposure! This will be so much fun!

I also have an Instagram page @janewinter_coloringbooks and I would love to share your amazing artwork there! I will also choose images from our FB Group for Instagram and tag you of course as the artist!

SOCIAL MEDIA LINKS:

FB page:
https://www.facebook.com/janewintercoloringbooks
FB Group "Jane Winter - Artwork":
https://www.facebook.com/groups/190076922695004/
Instagram:
https://www.instagram.com/janewinter_coloringbooks/

Jane Winter

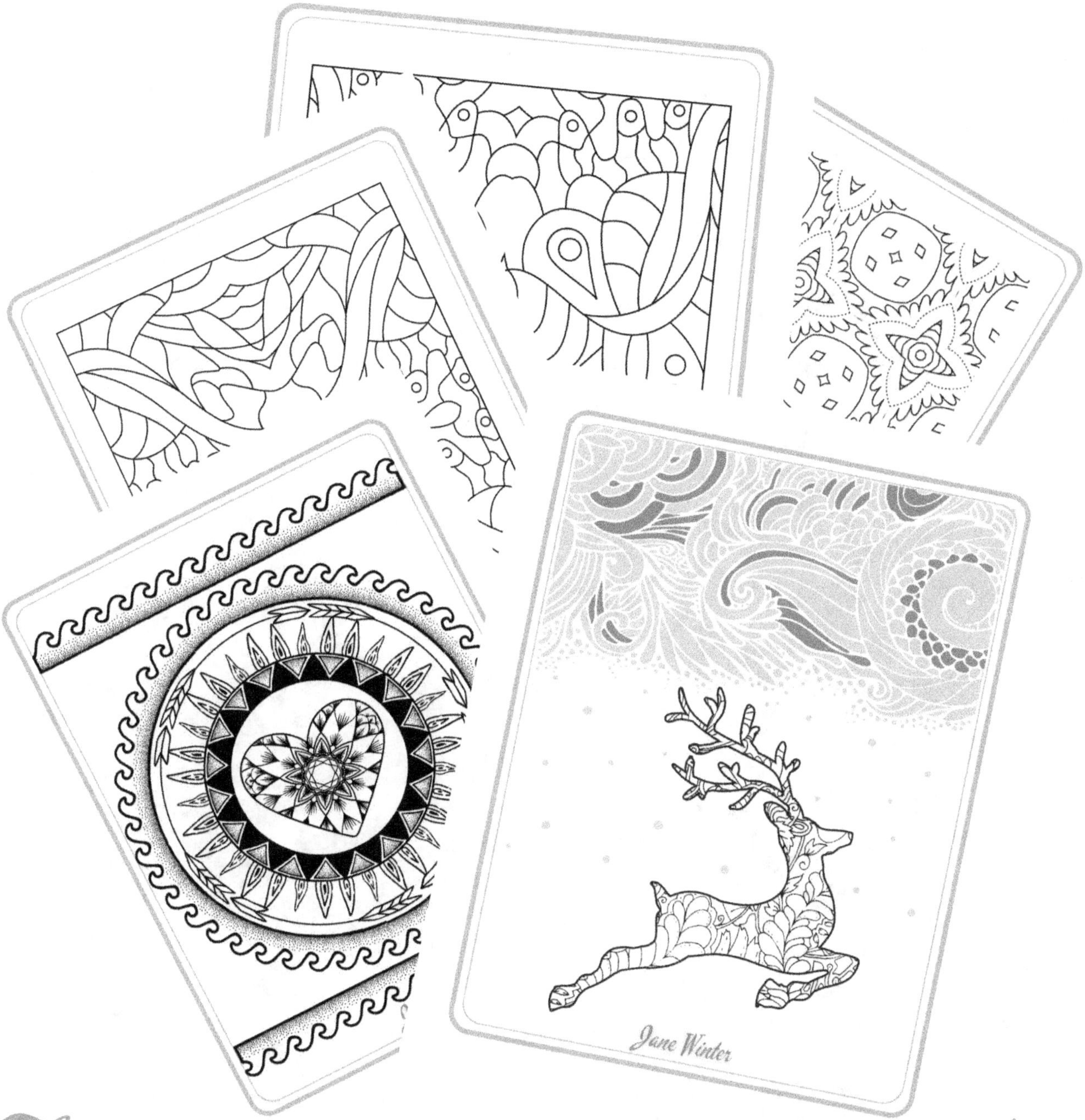

Free COLORING PAGES every month!

https://jane-winter.com/free/

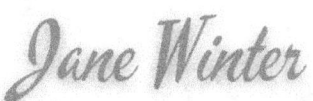

Color test page

Jane Winter

This page is left
blank intentionally
to avoid any bleed-through
on the paper.

Jane Winter

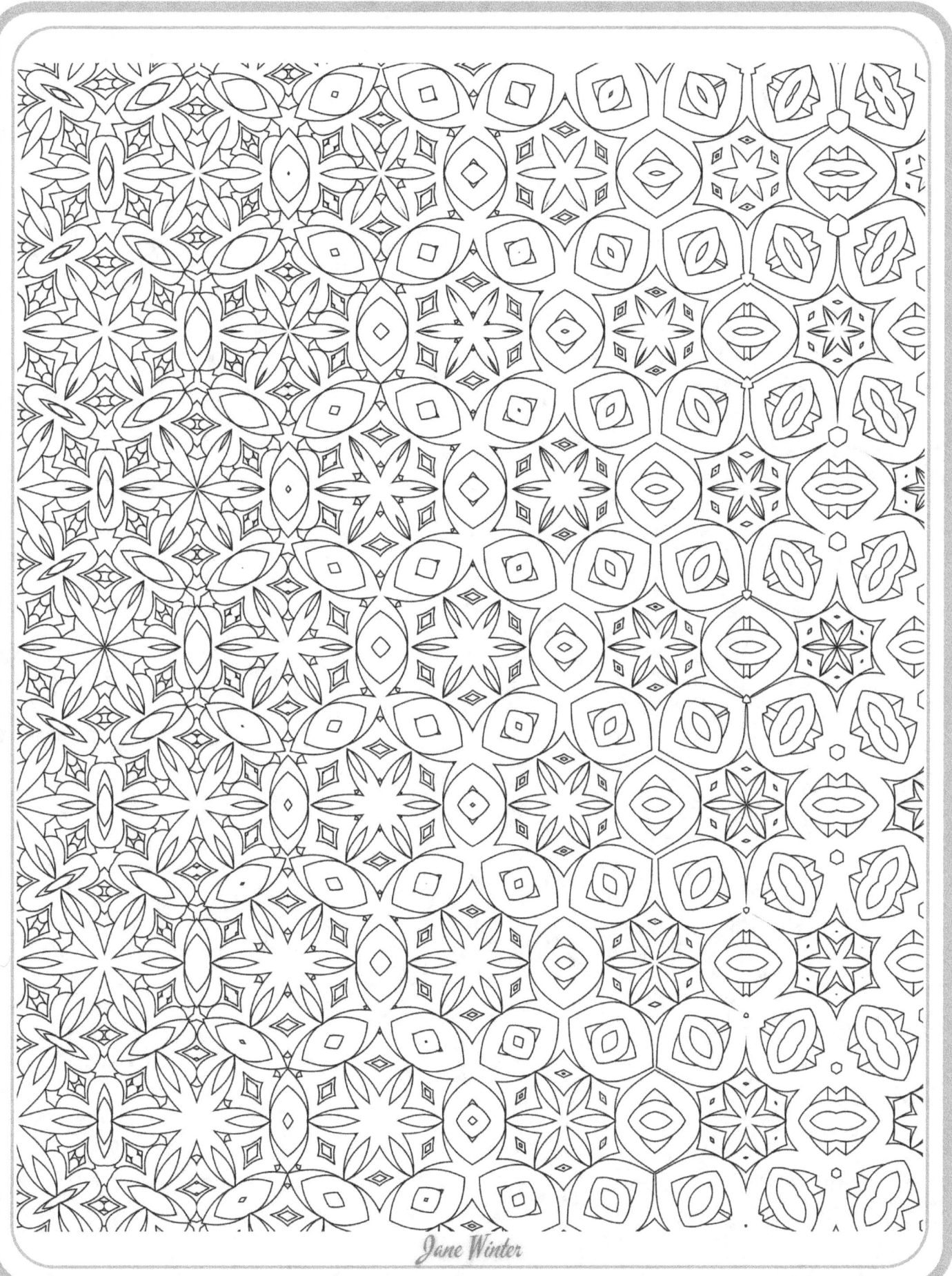
Jane Winter

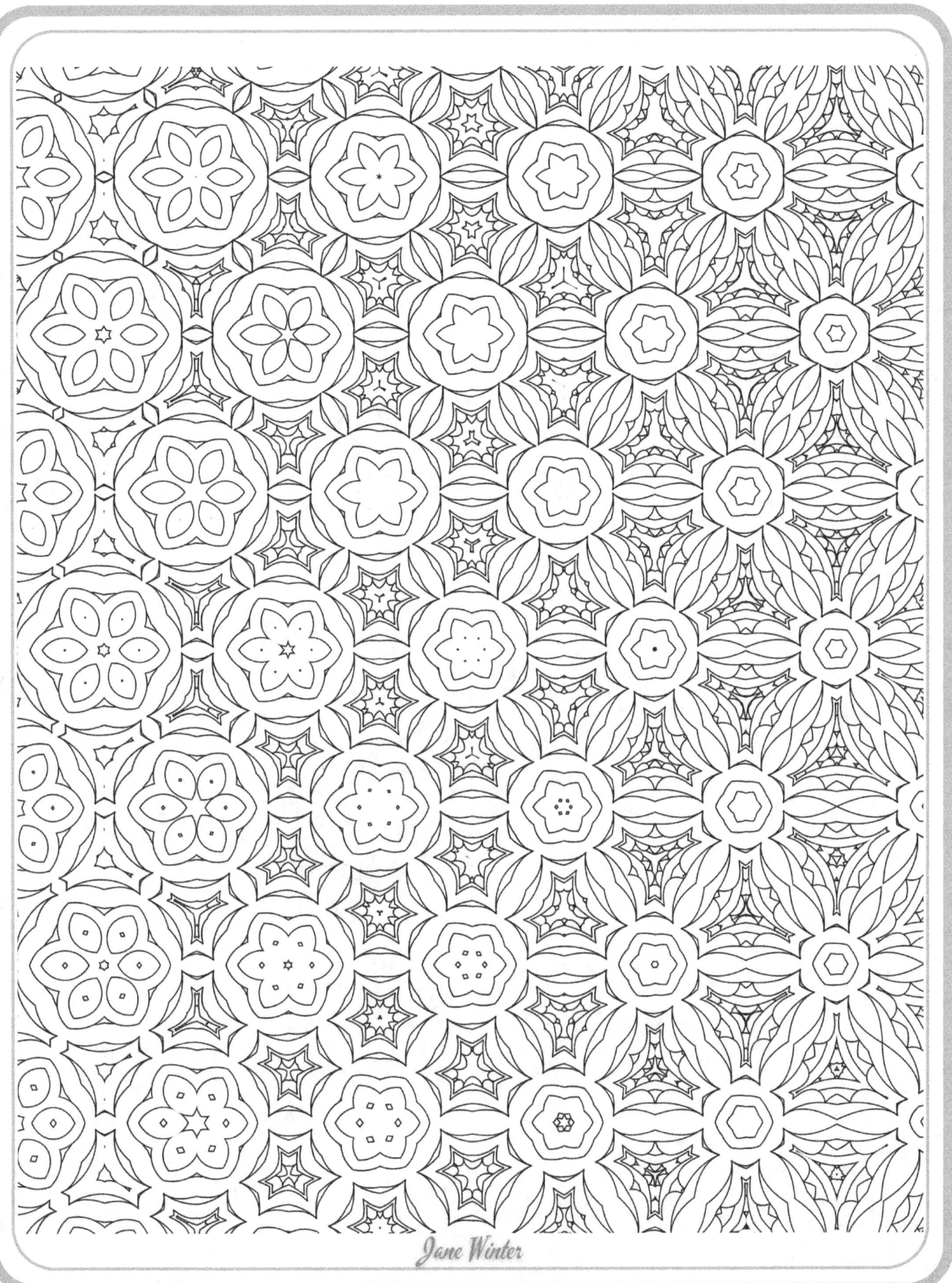

Jane Winter

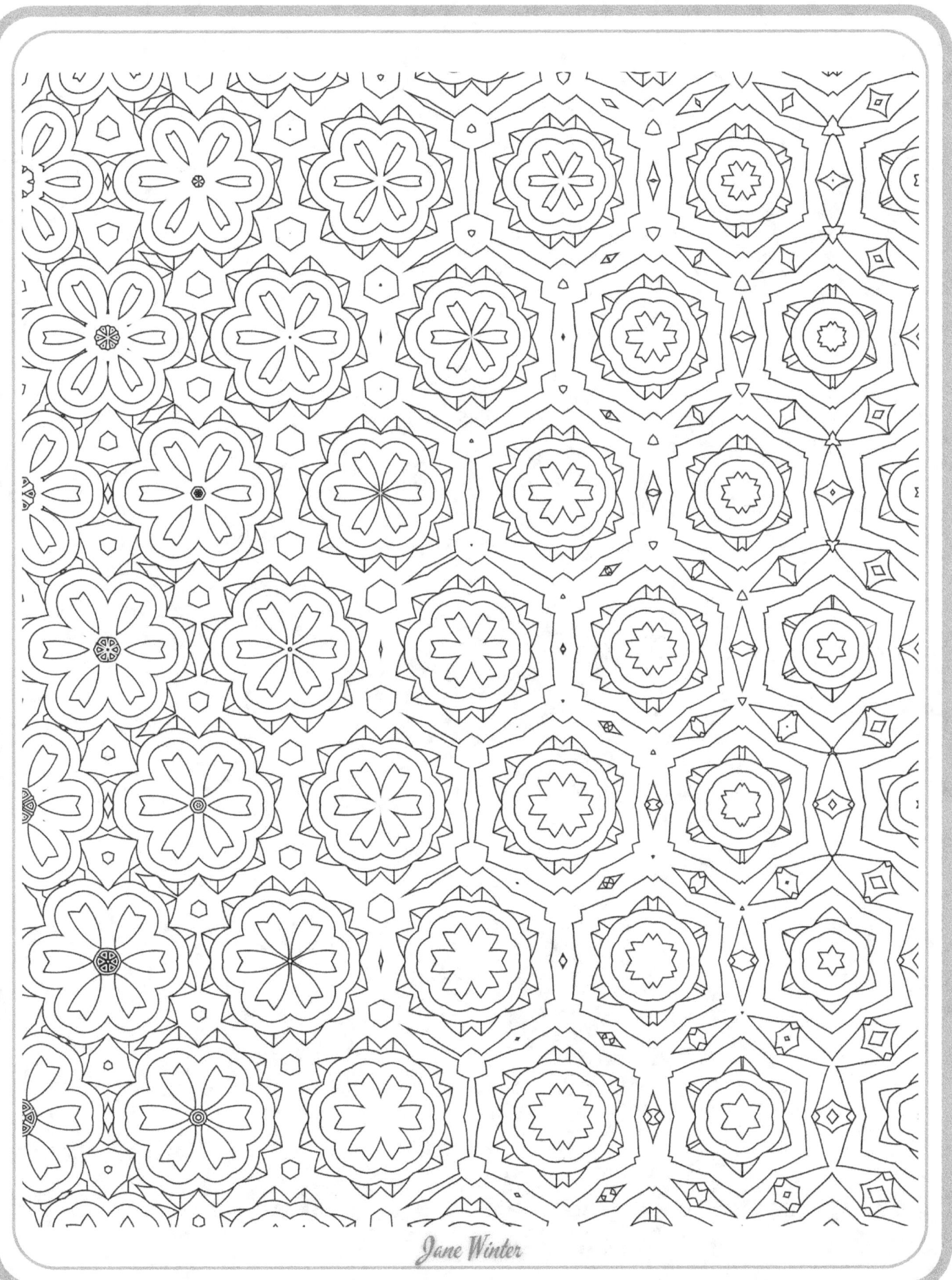

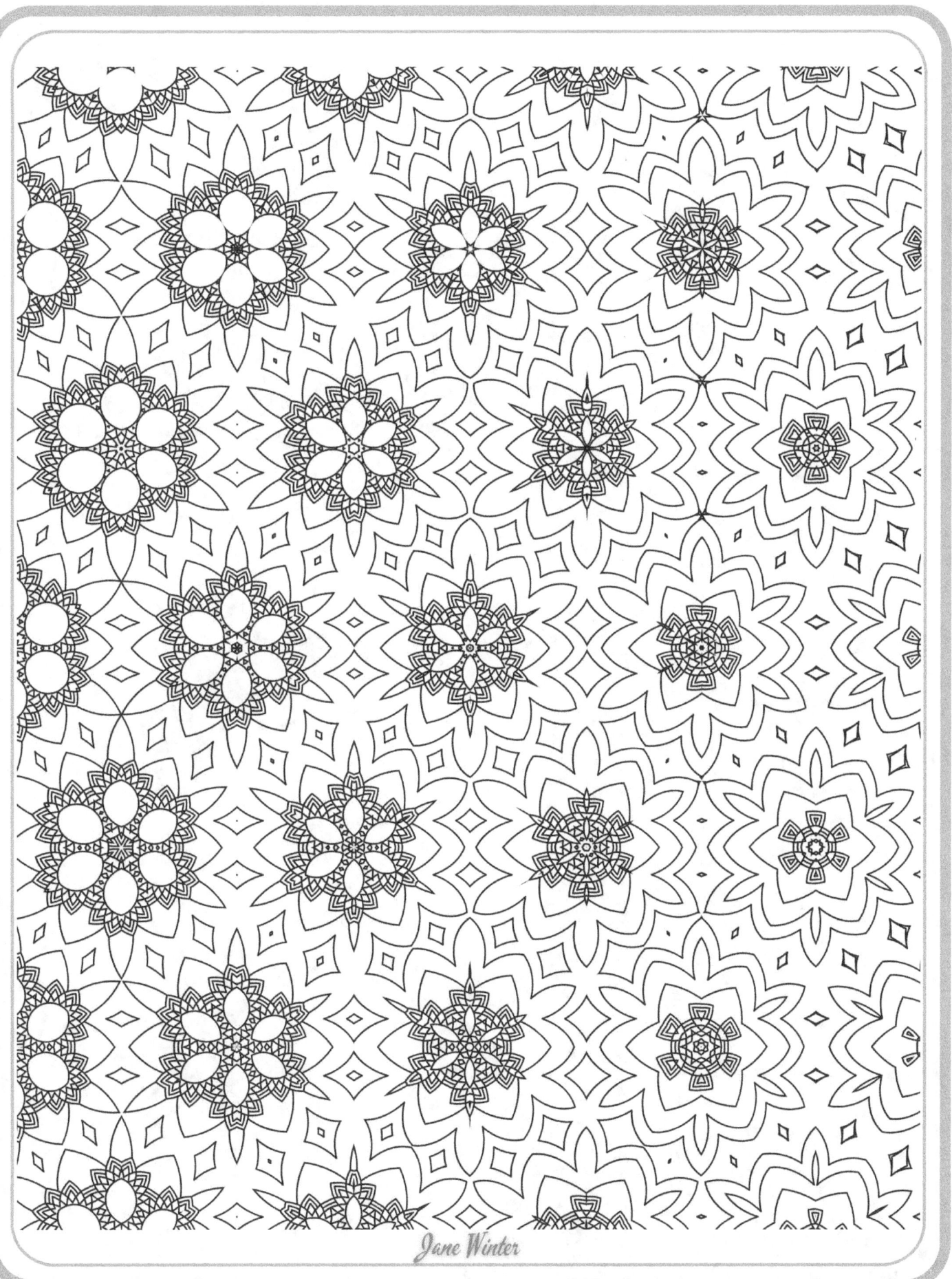

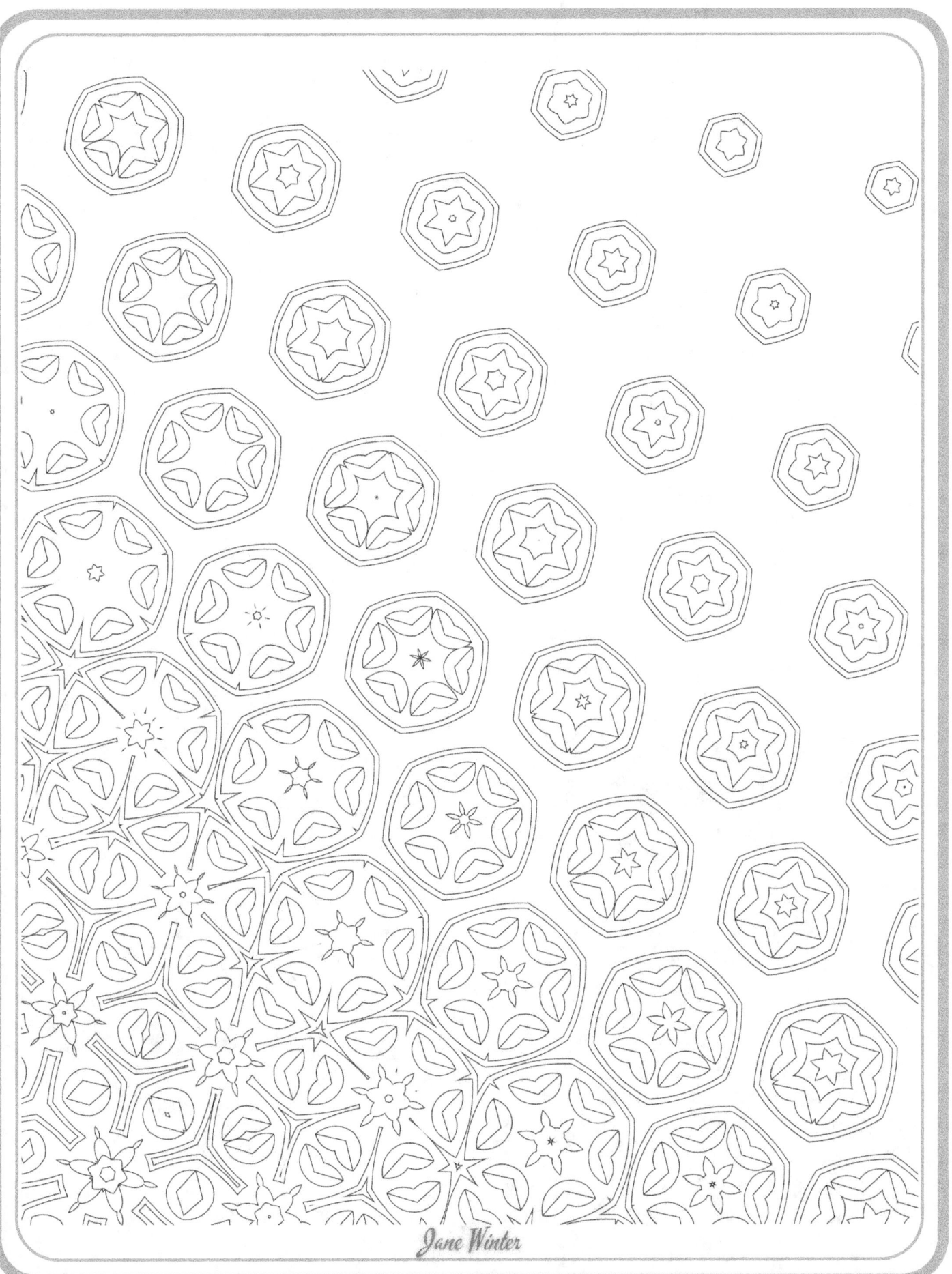

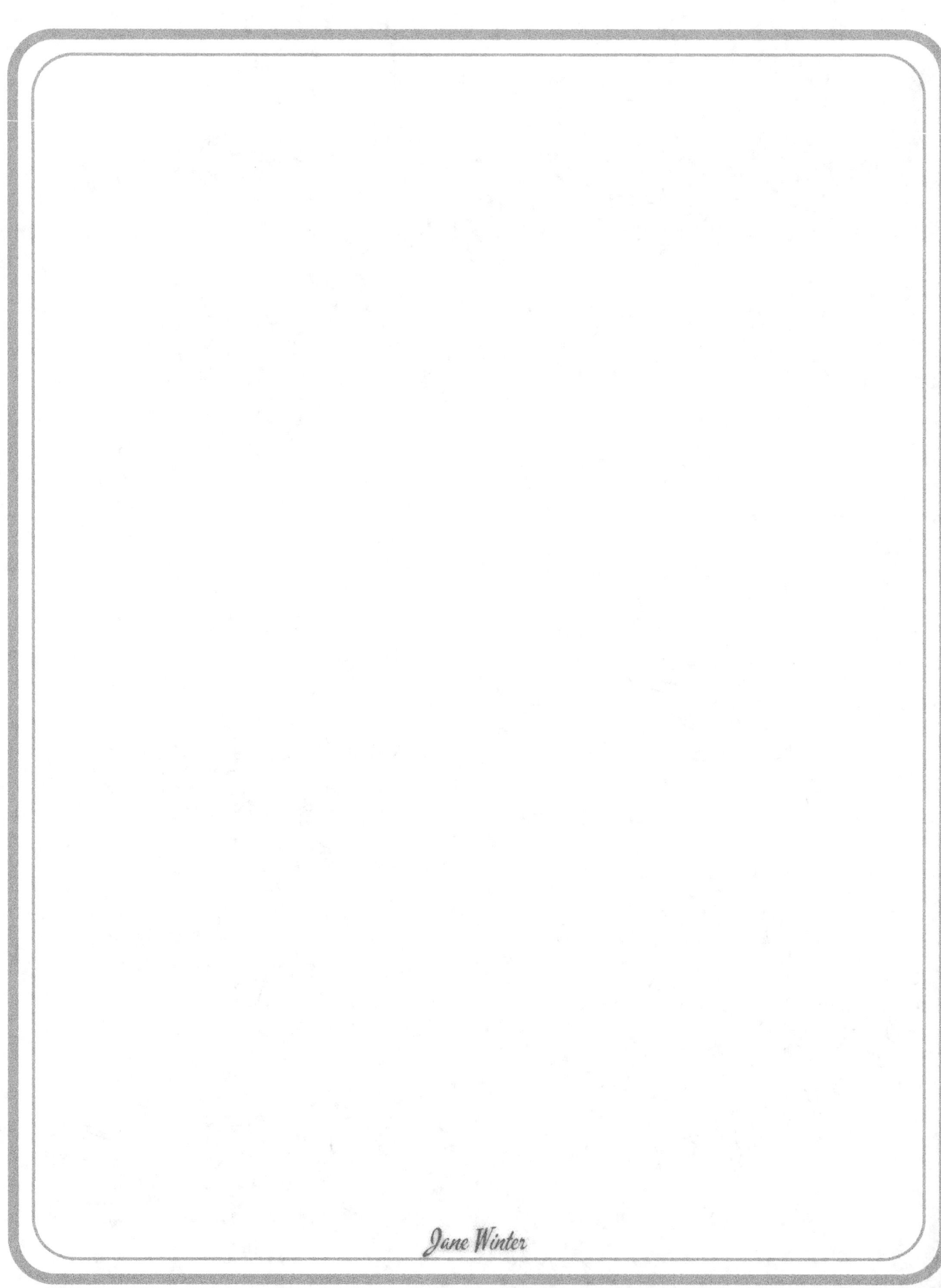

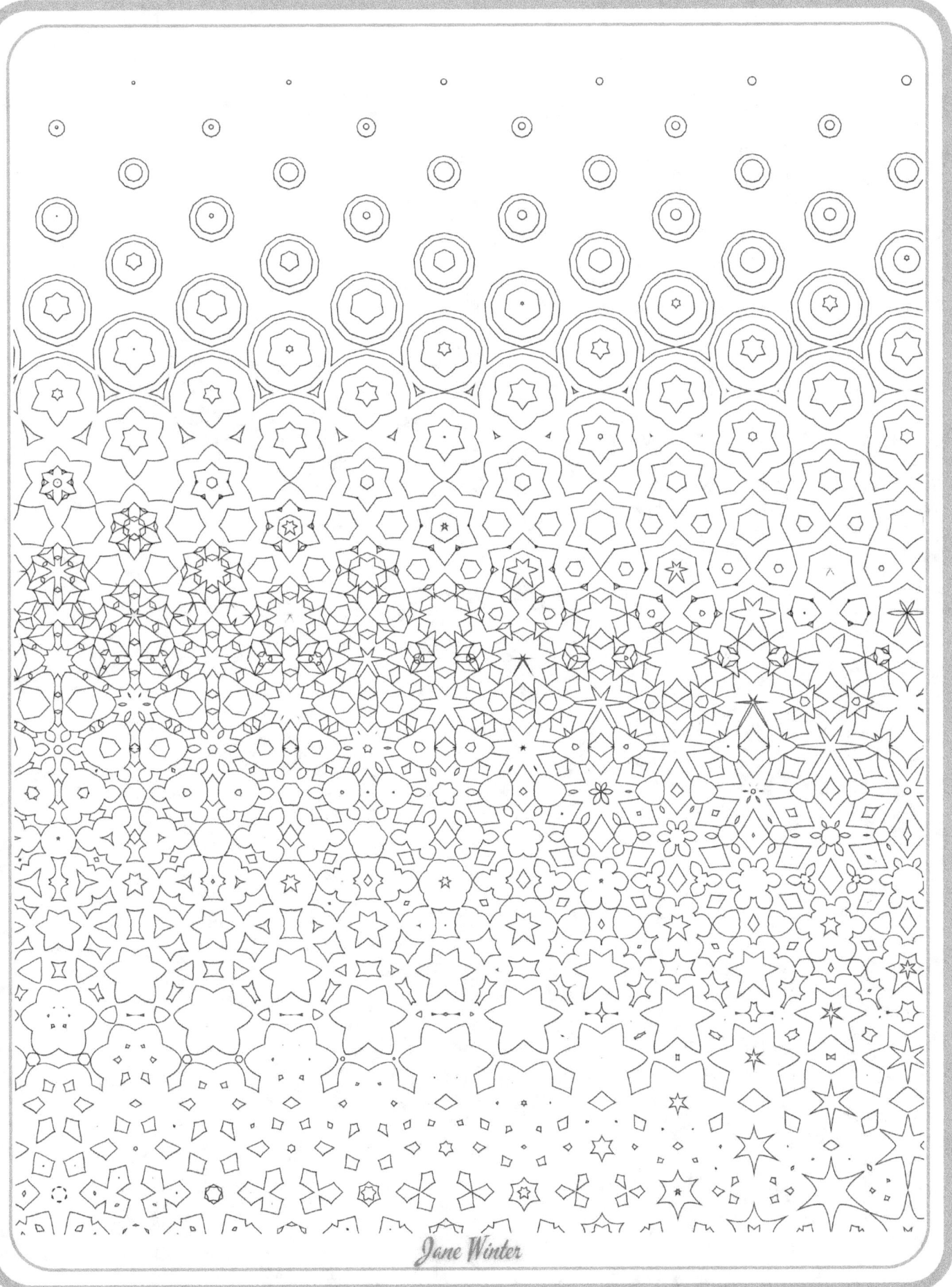

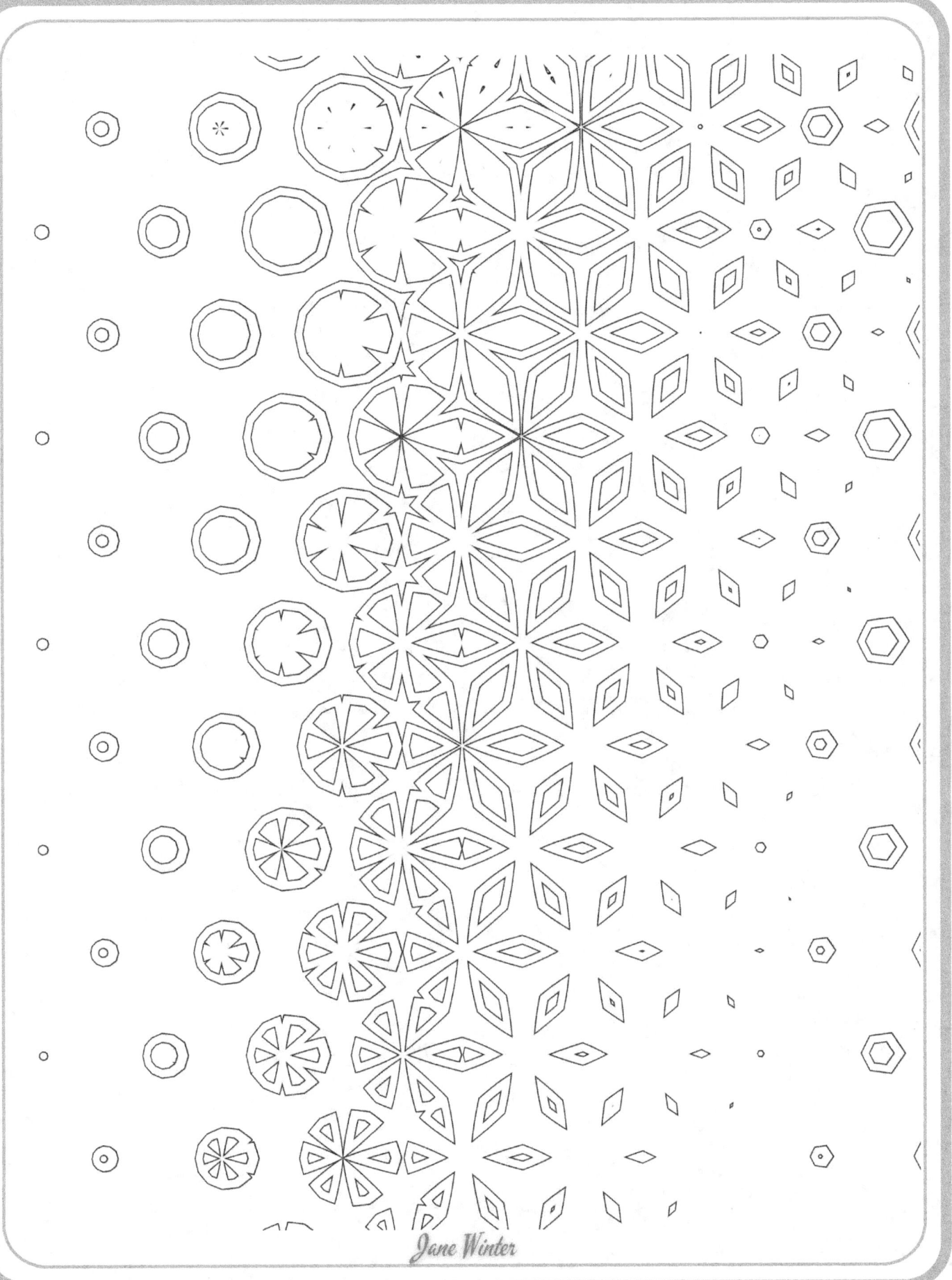

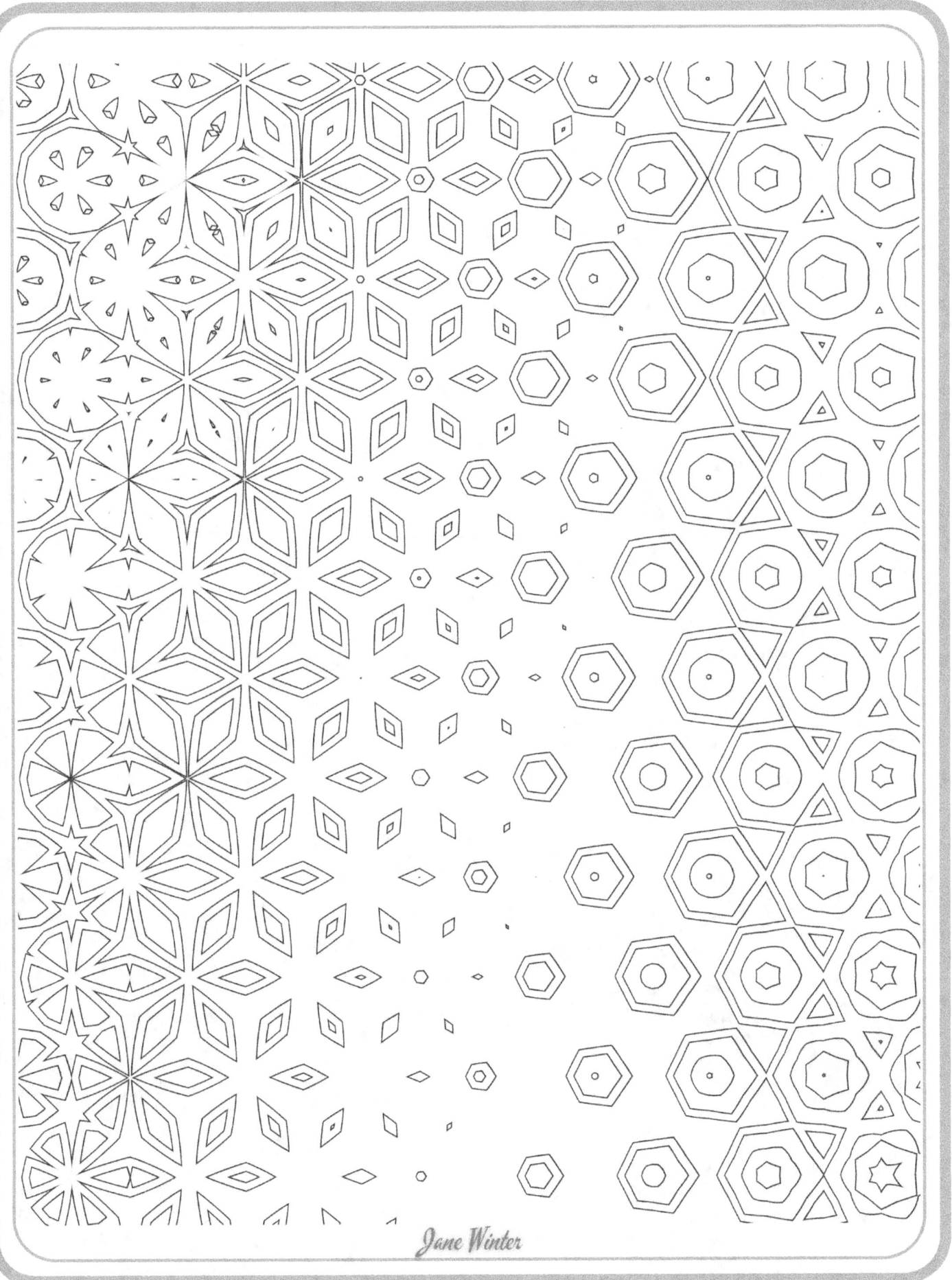

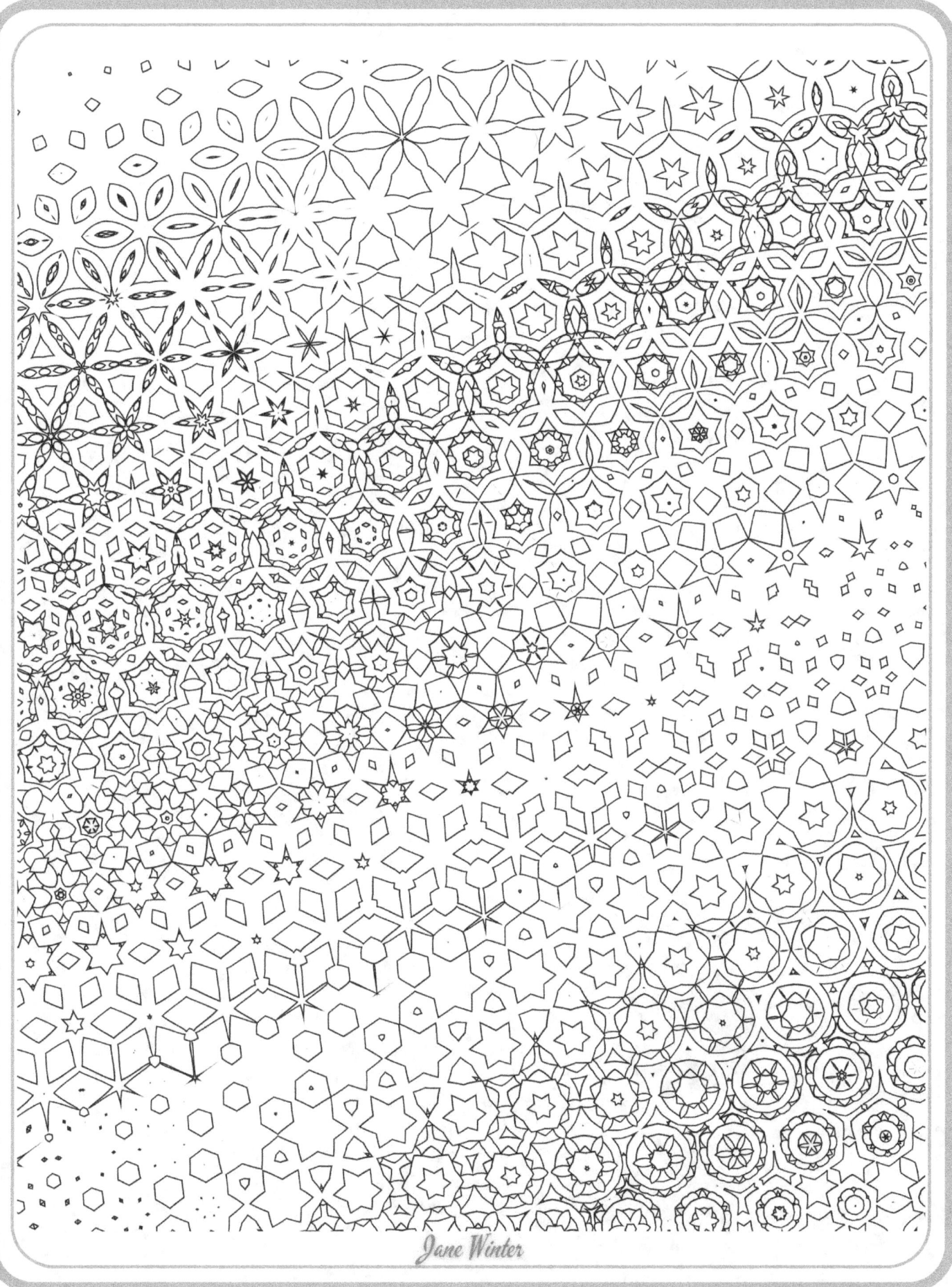

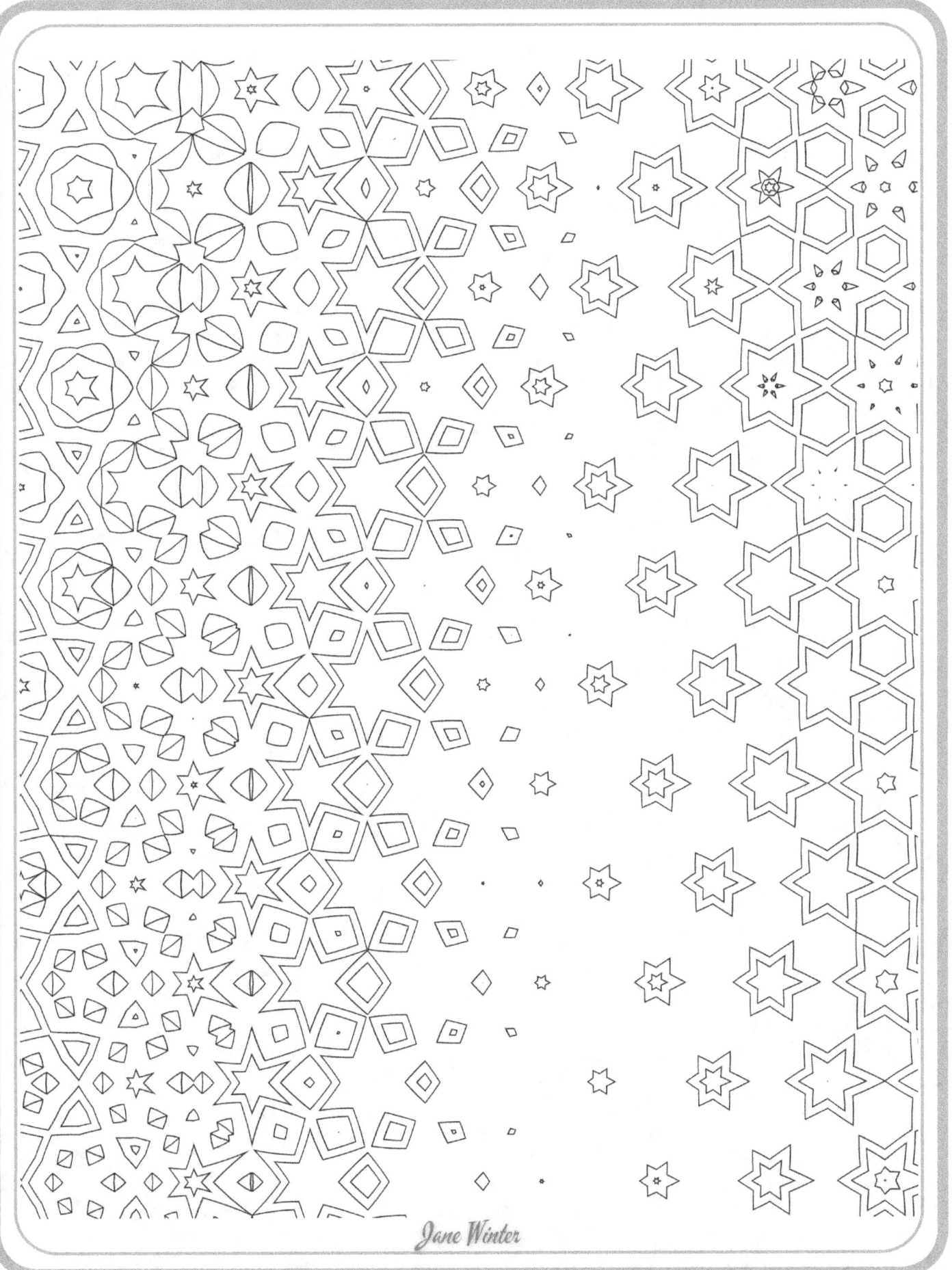

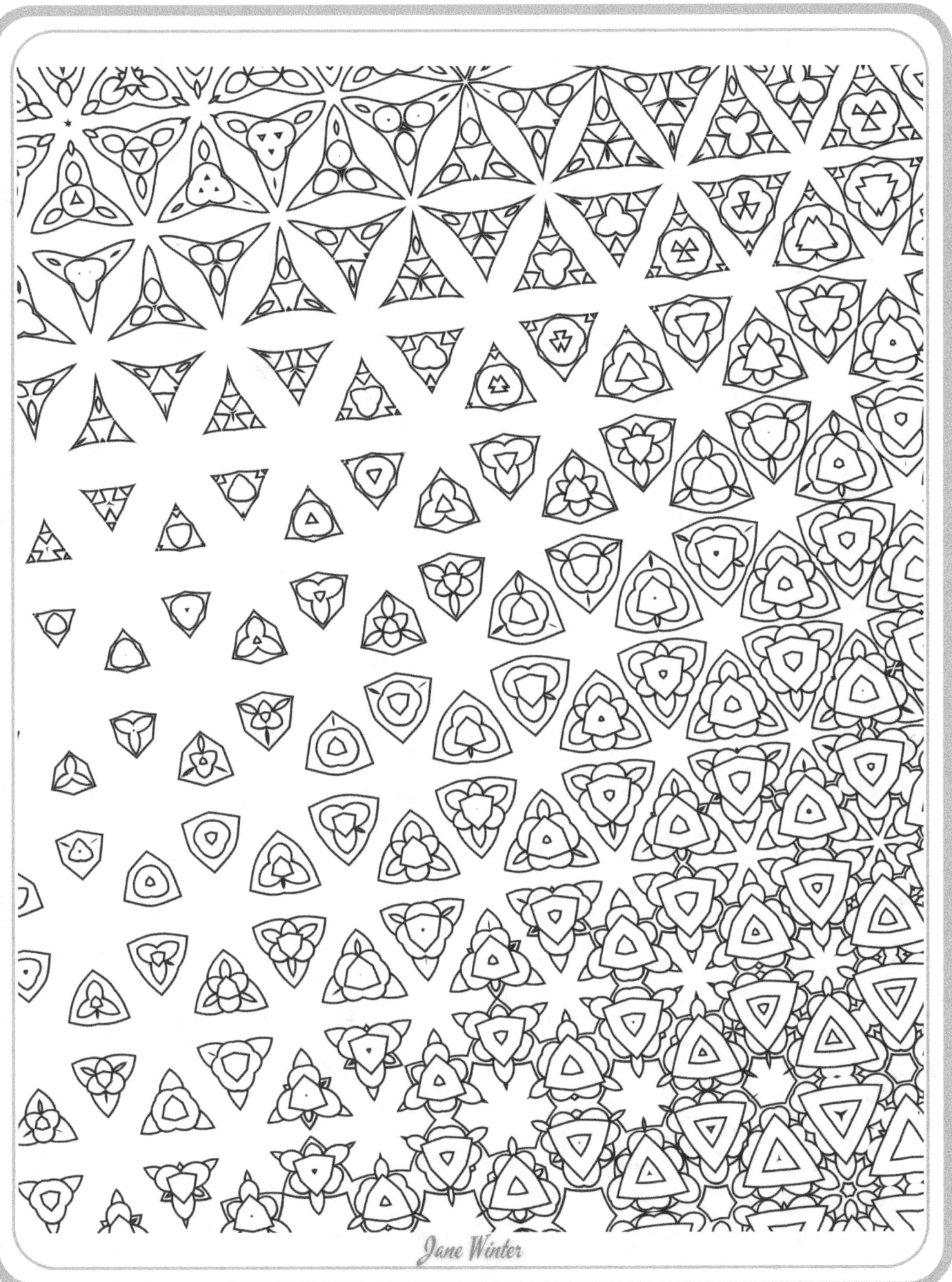

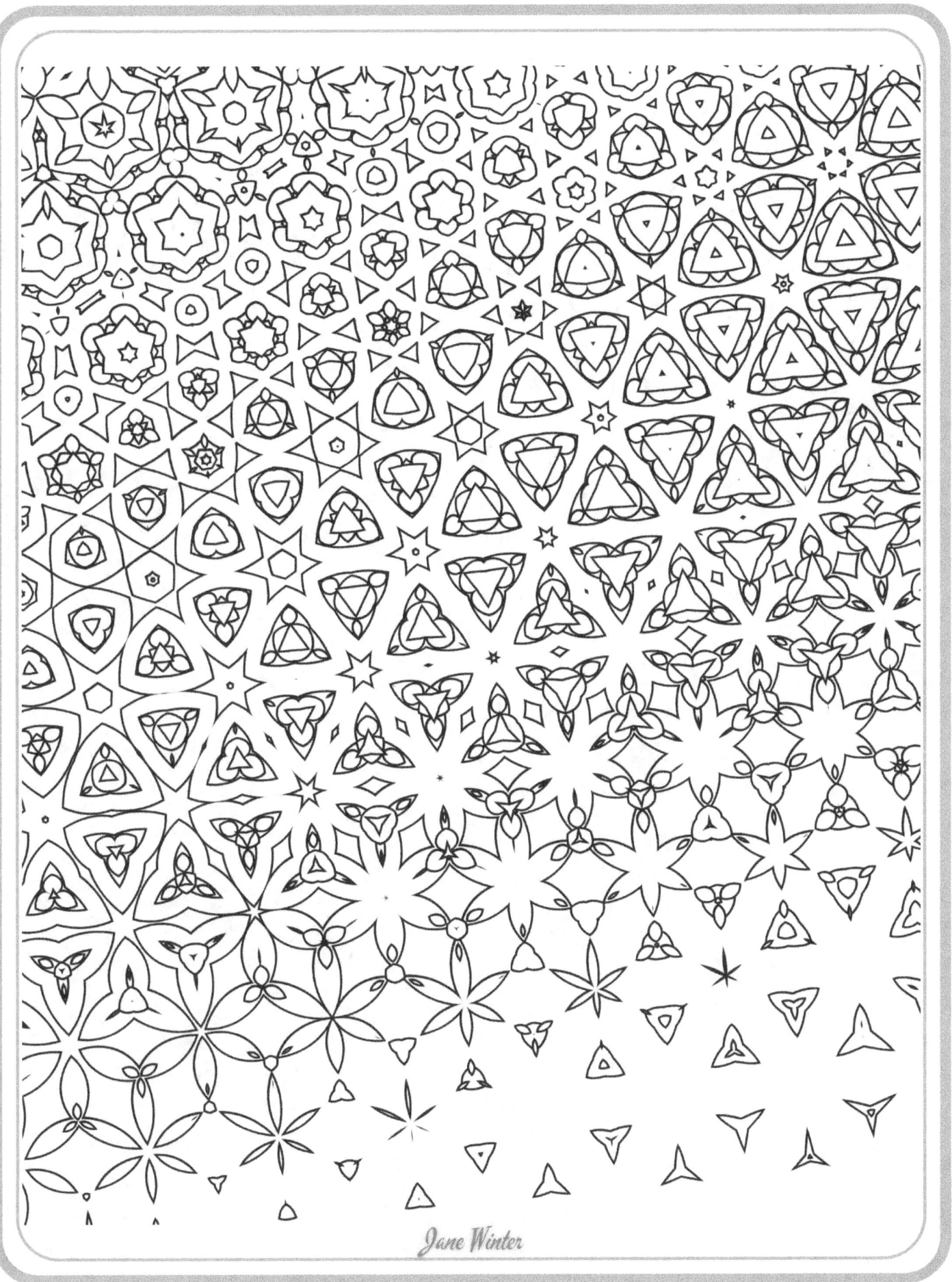

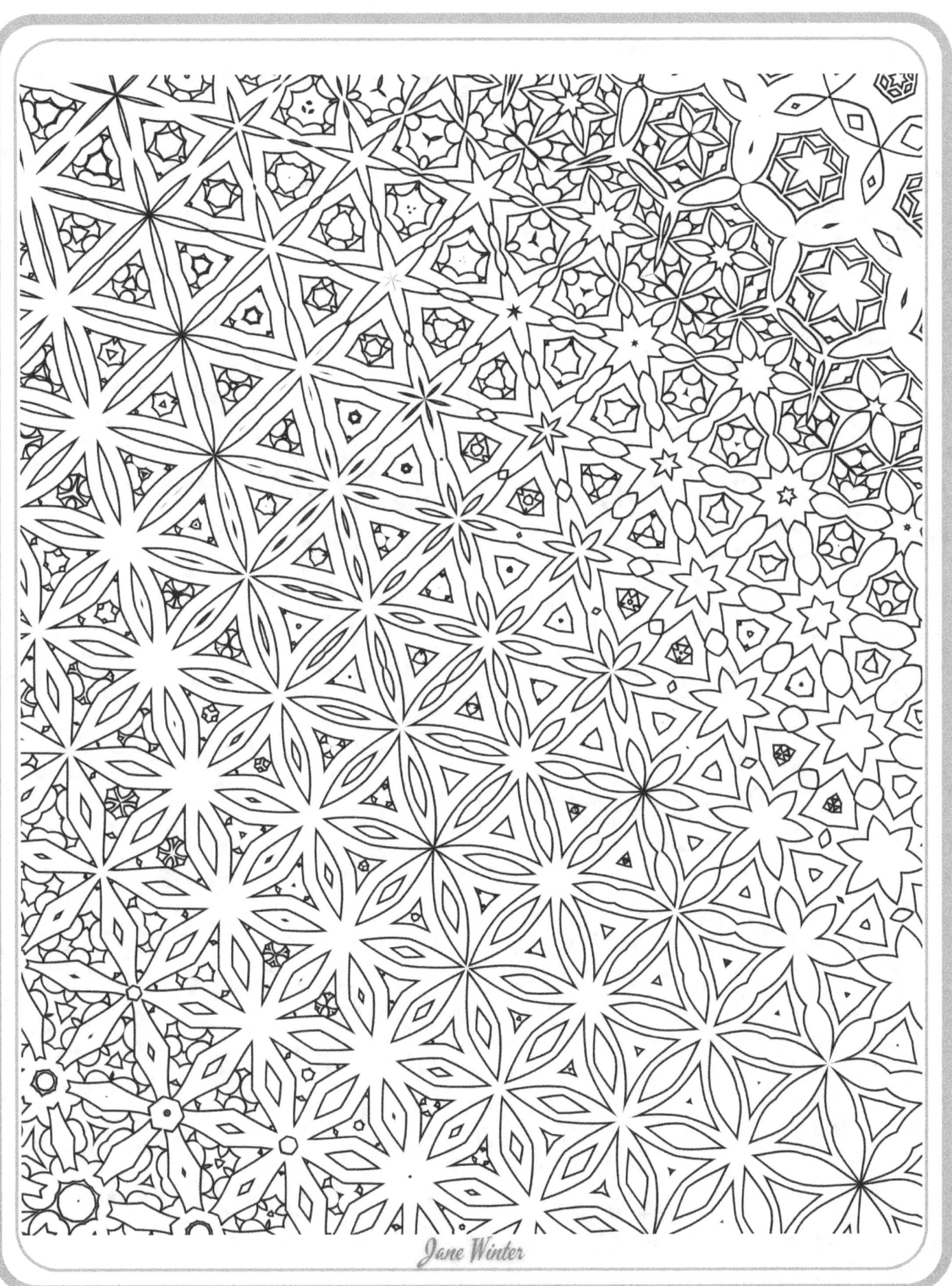

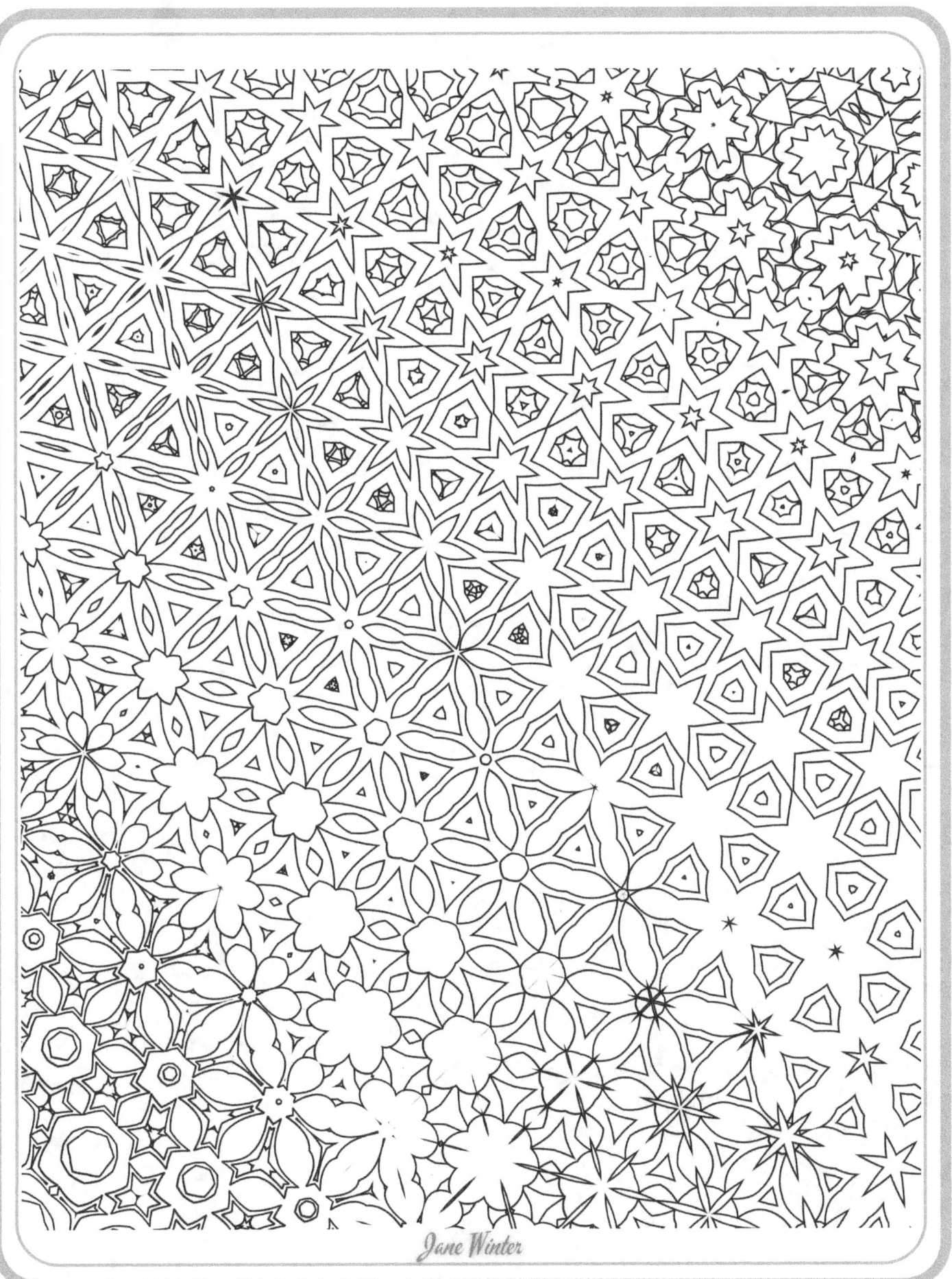
Jane Winter

Jane Winter

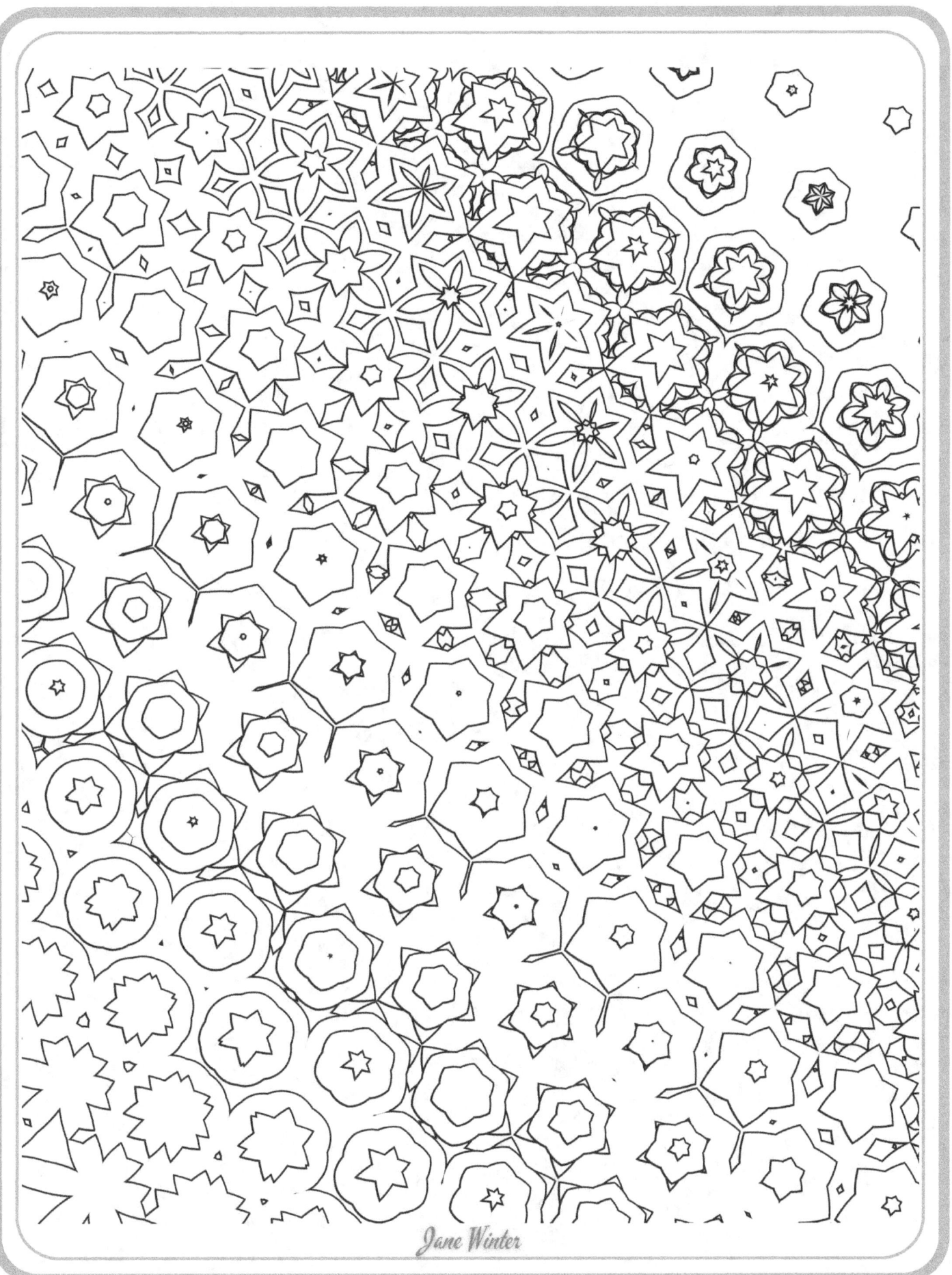

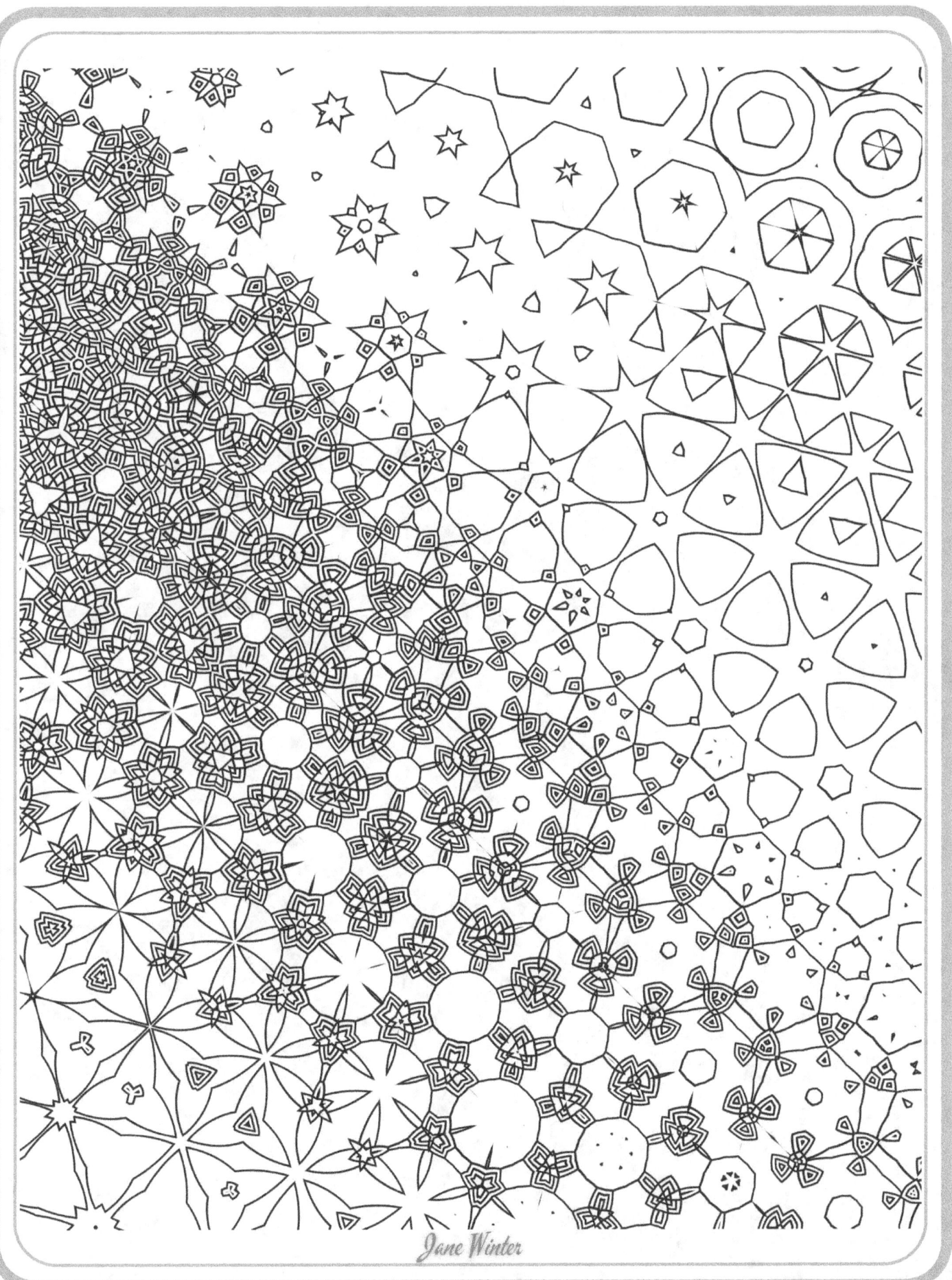

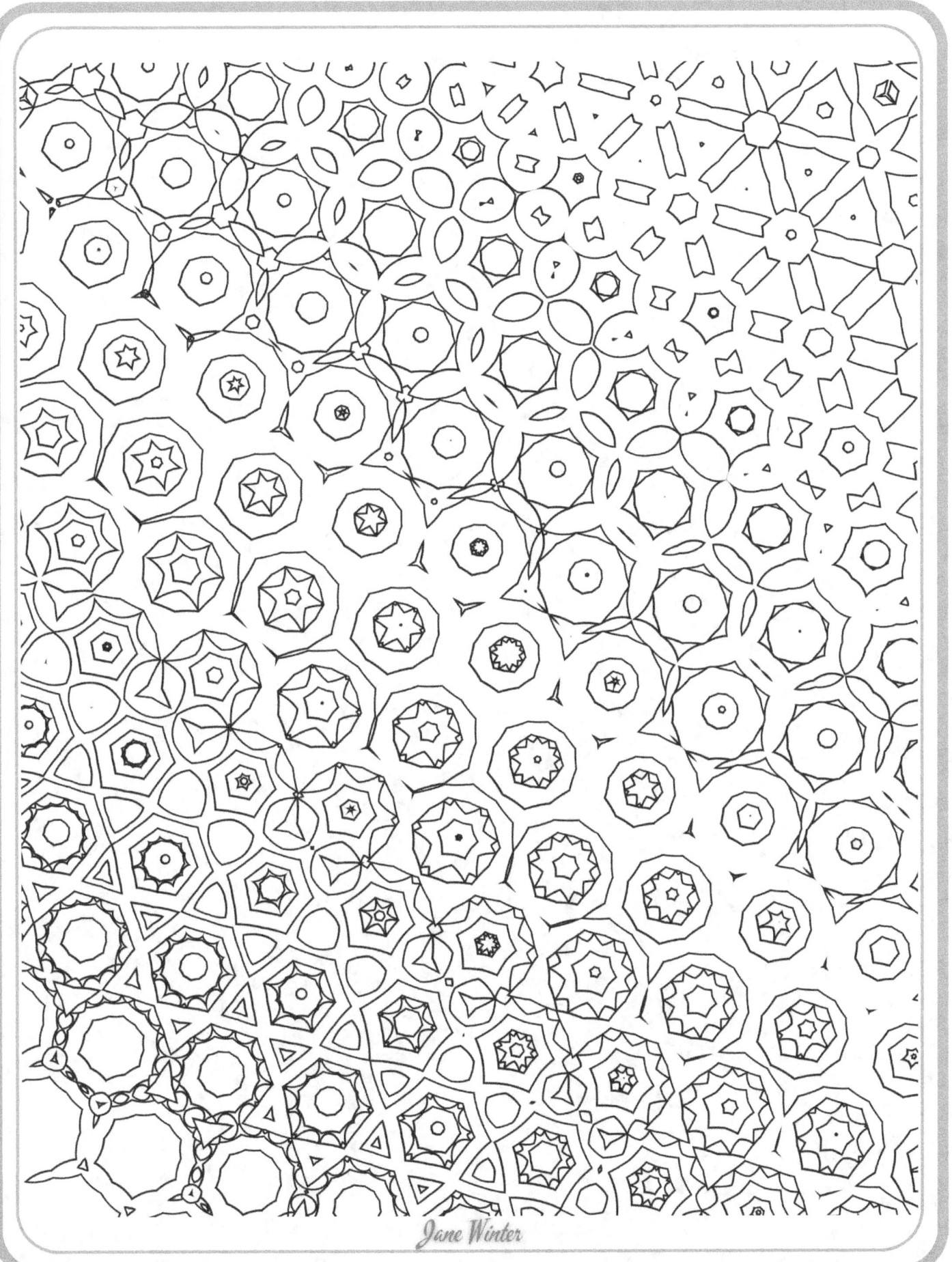

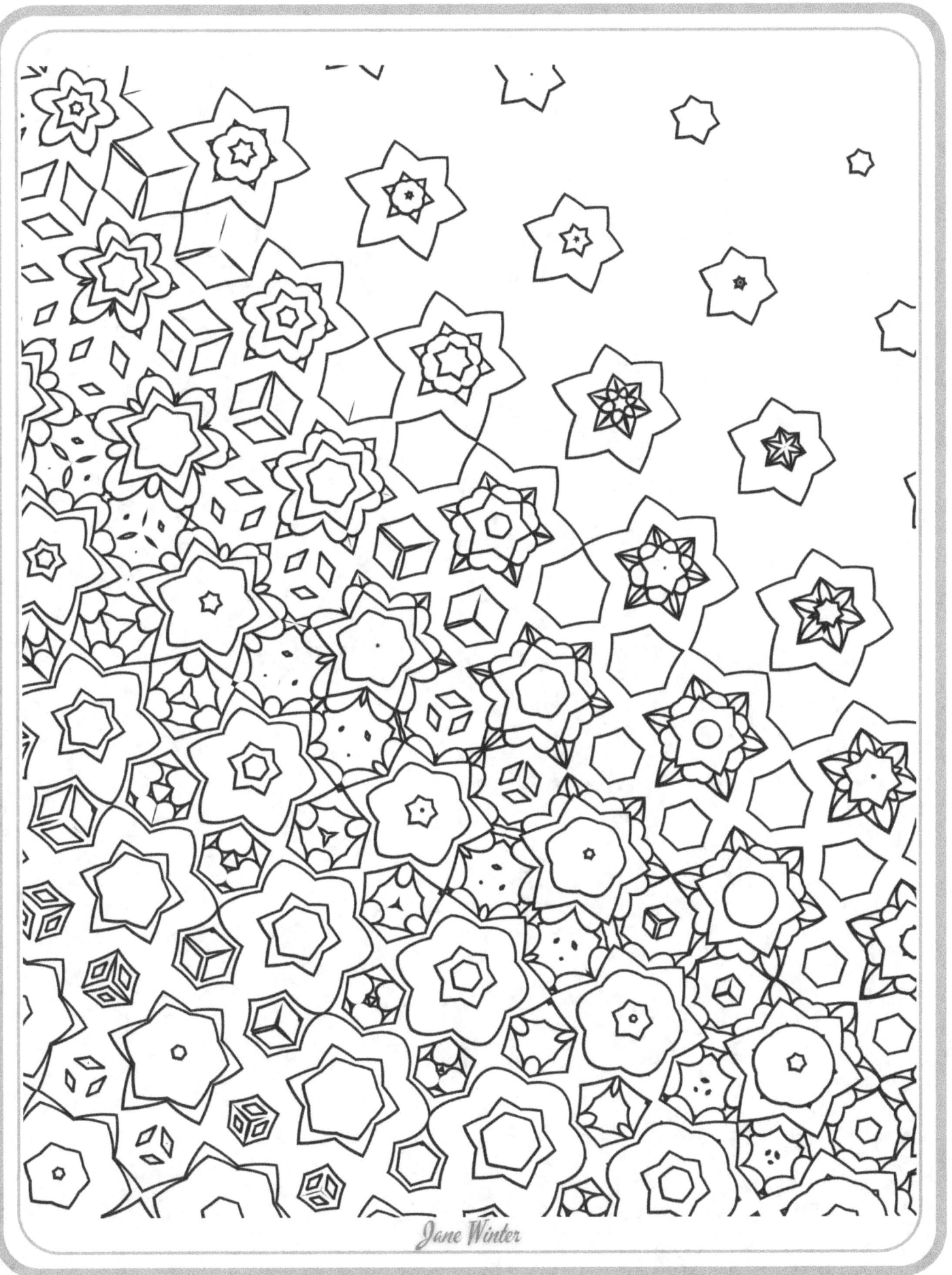

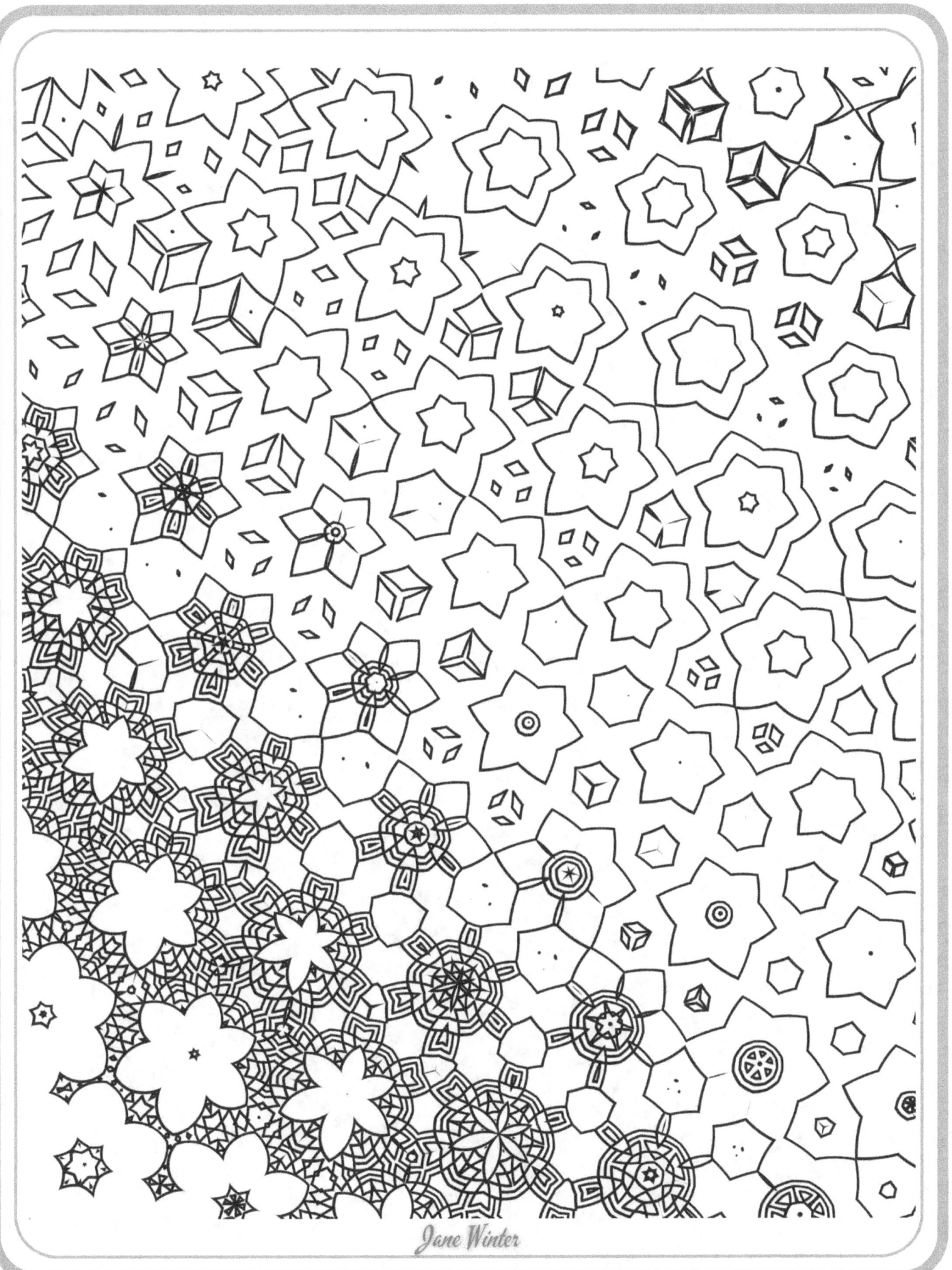

Jane Winter

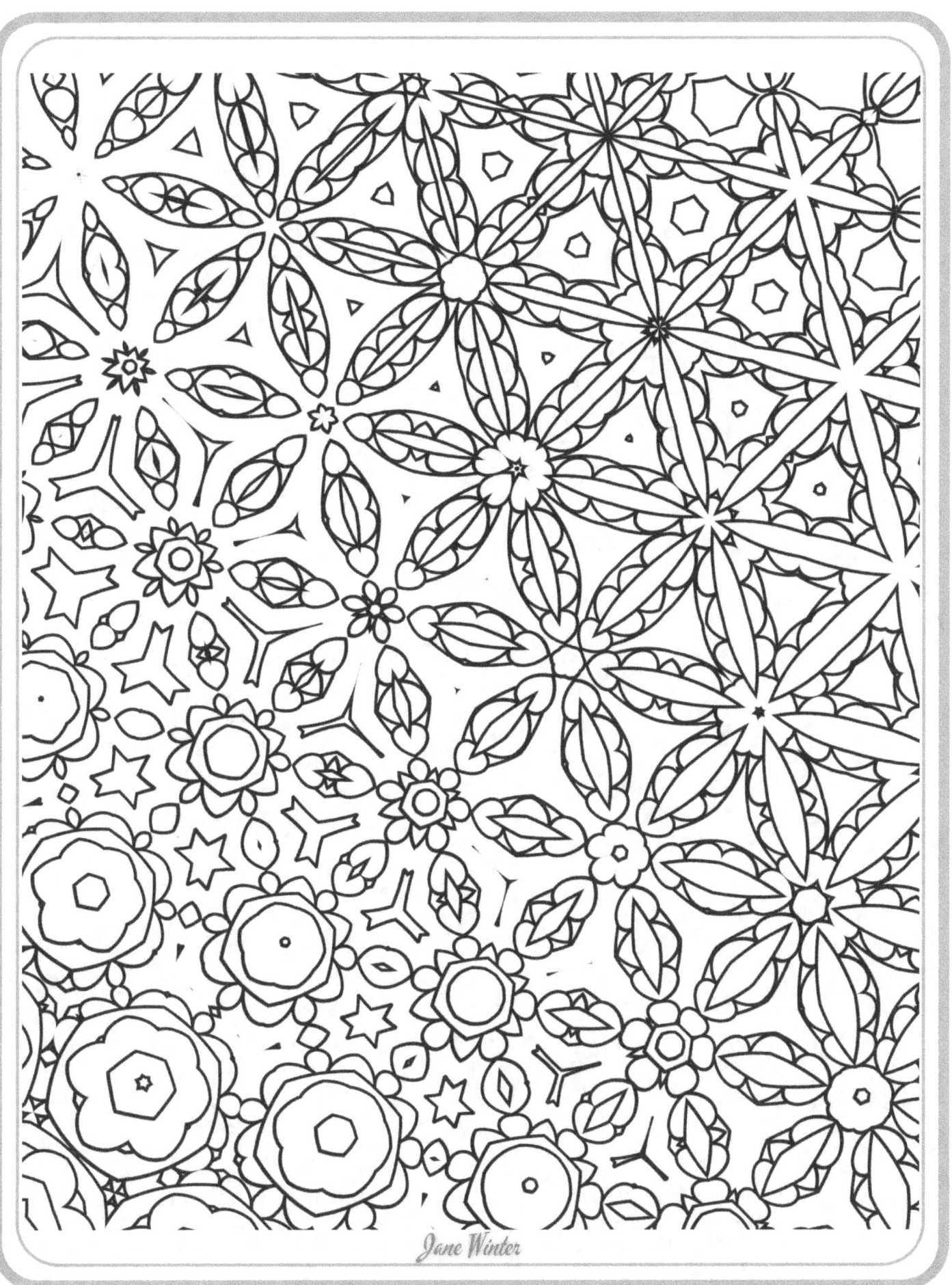

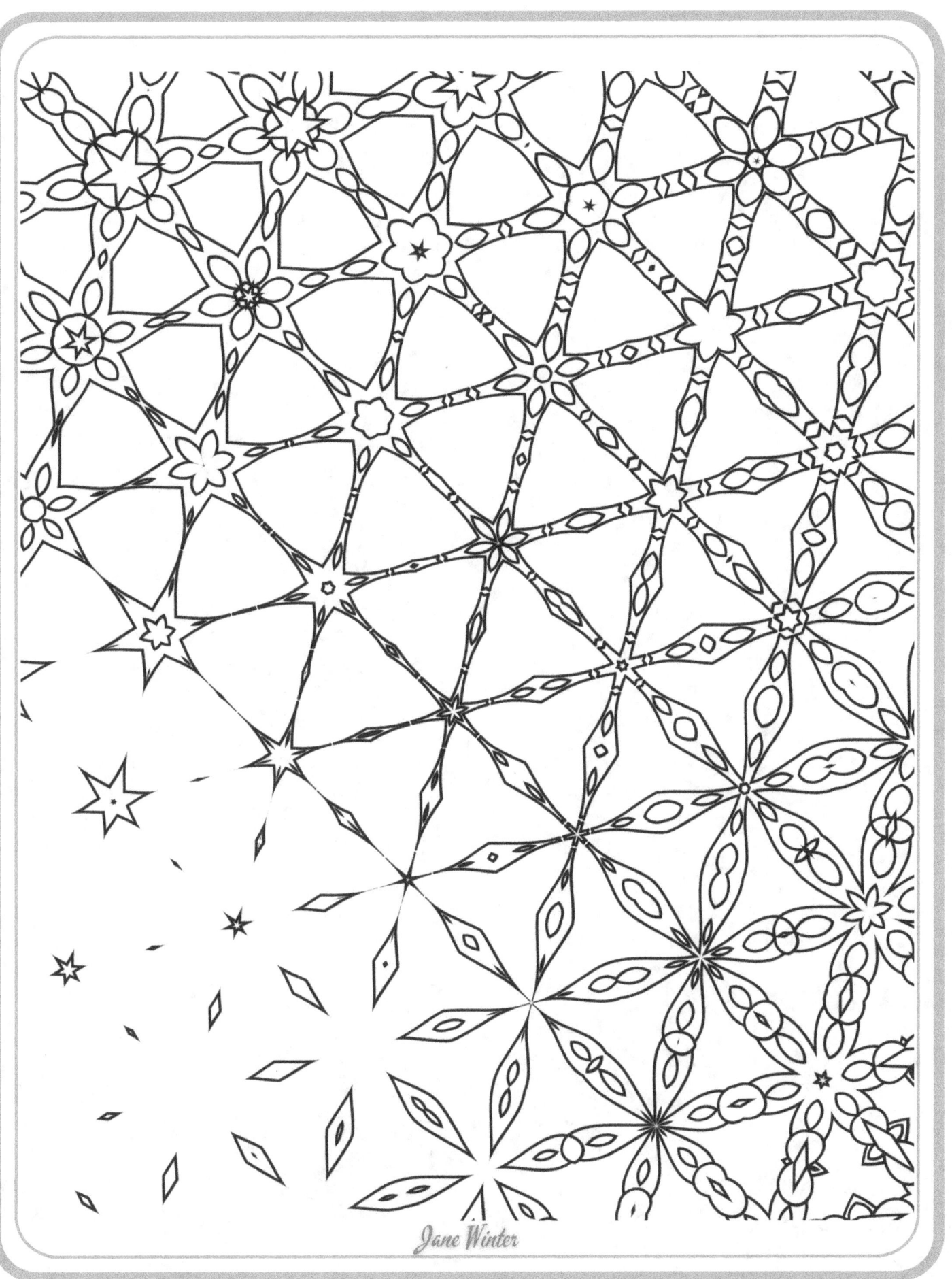

Jane Winter

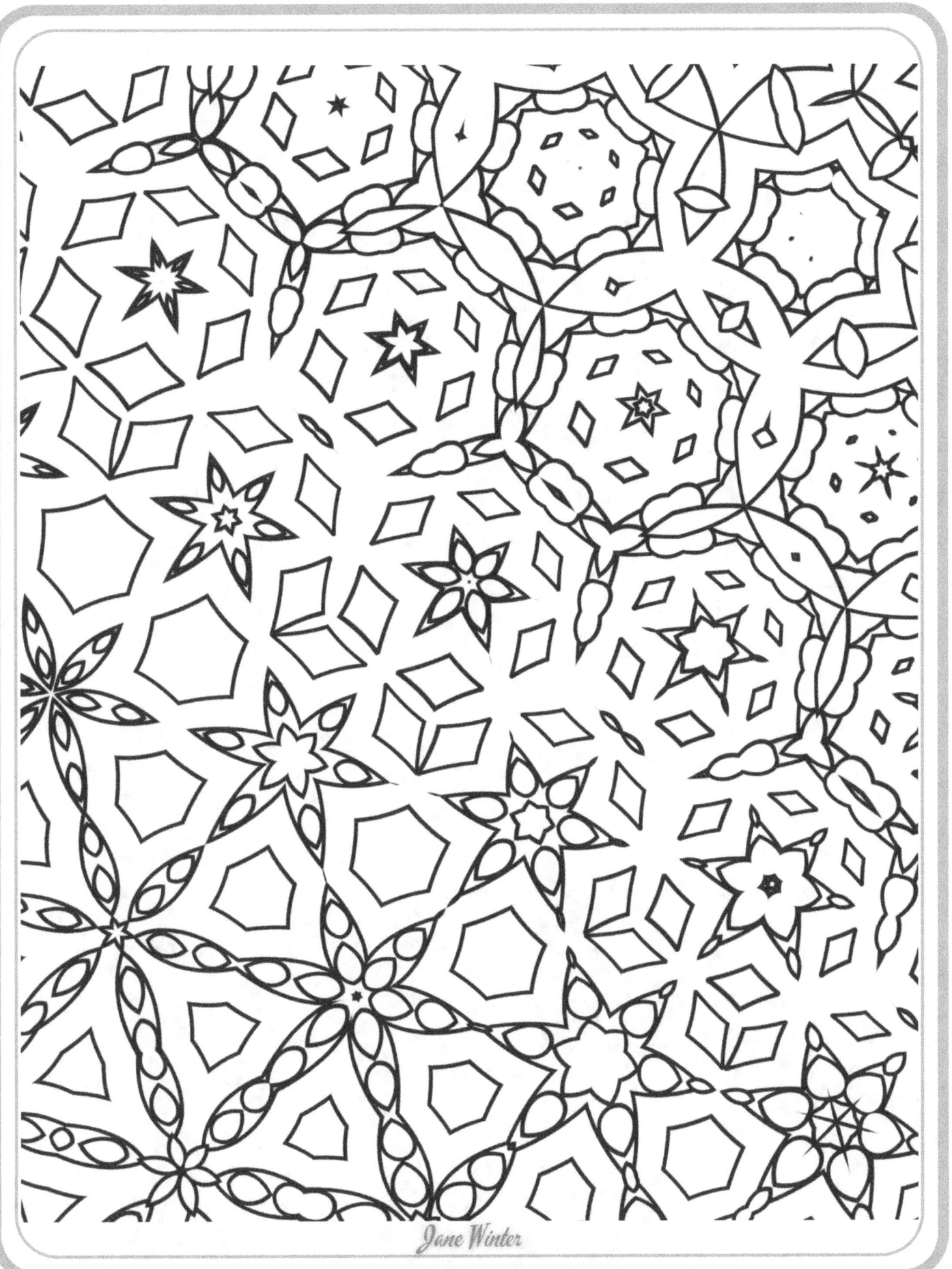

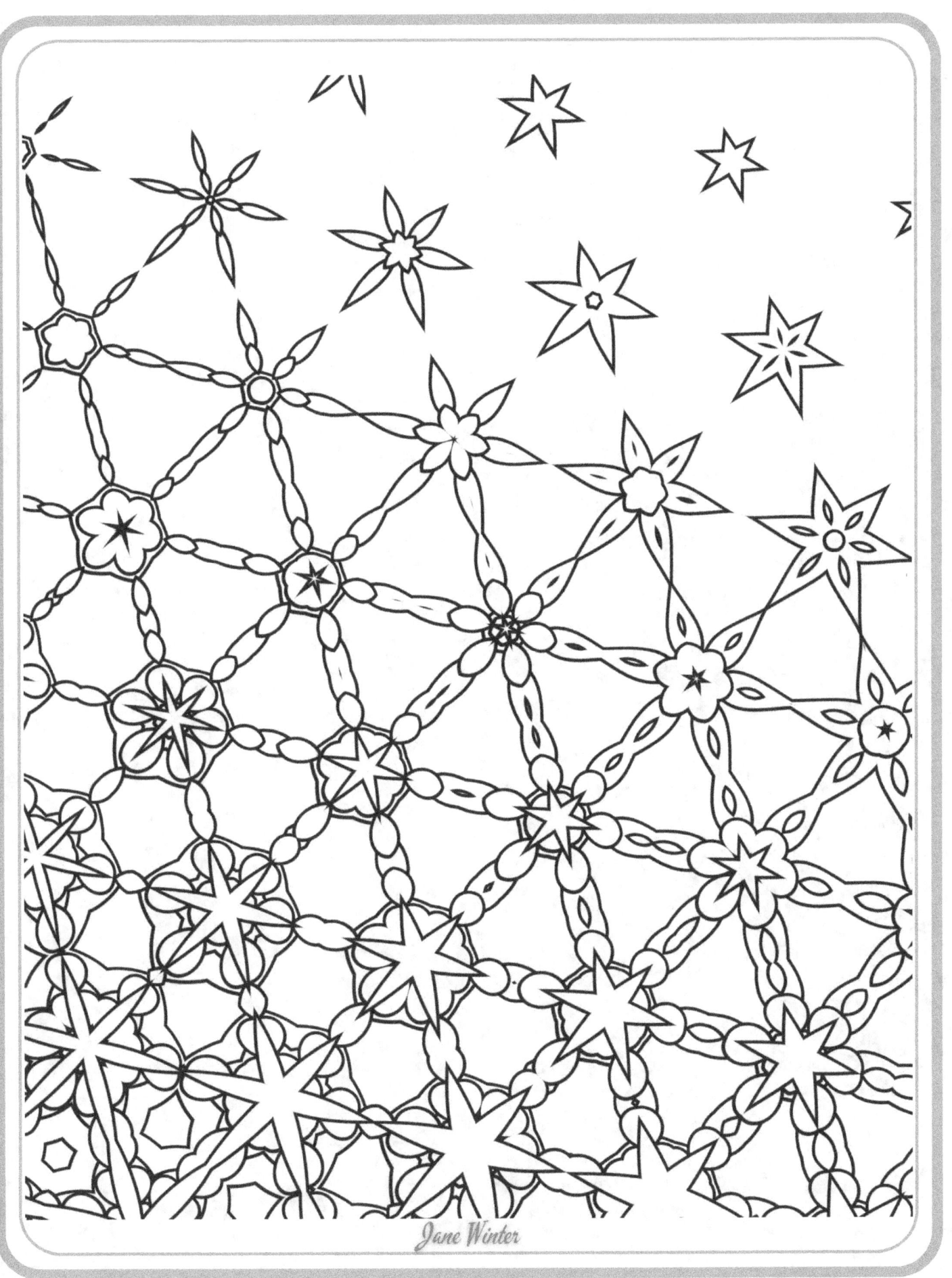

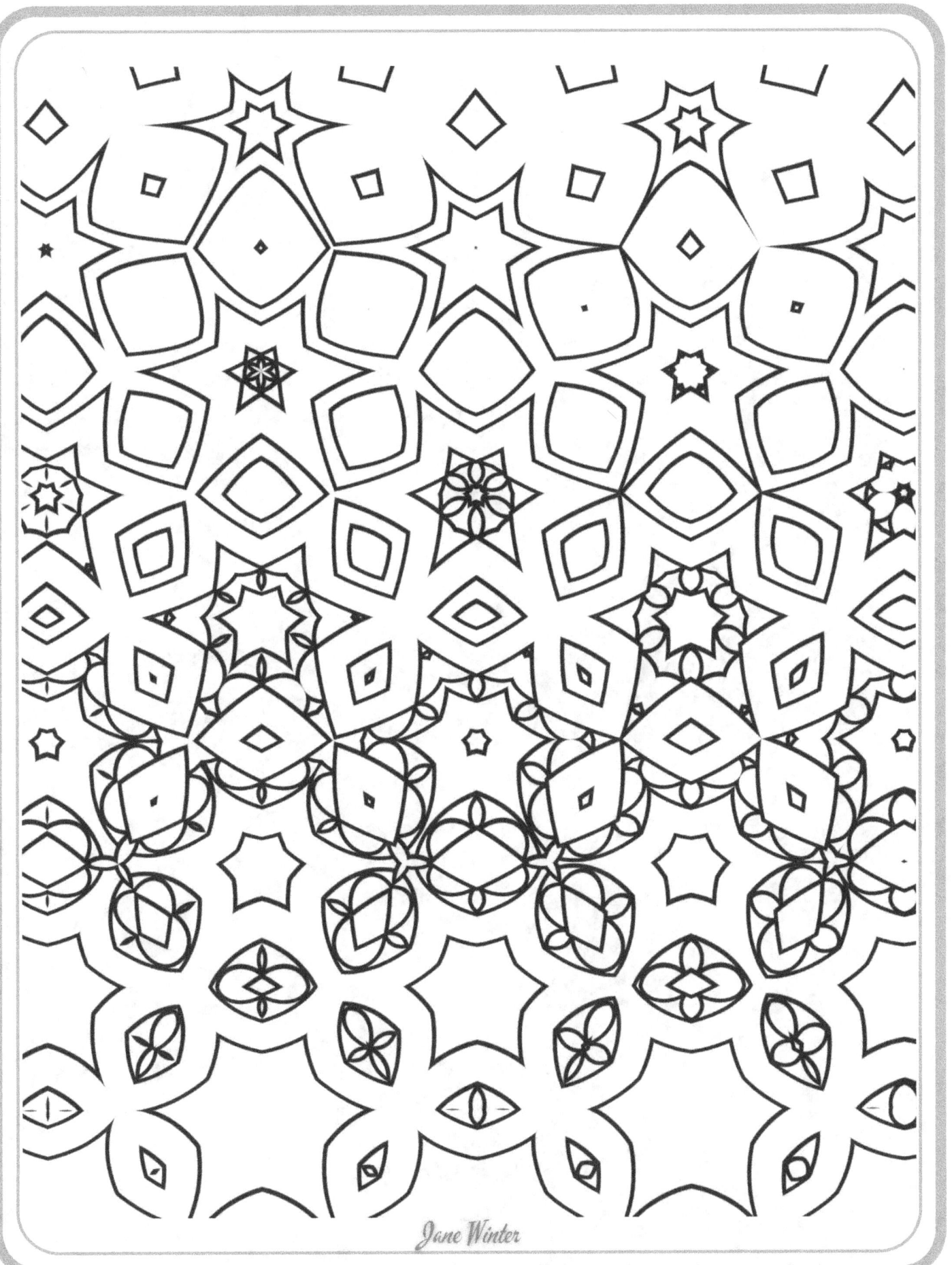

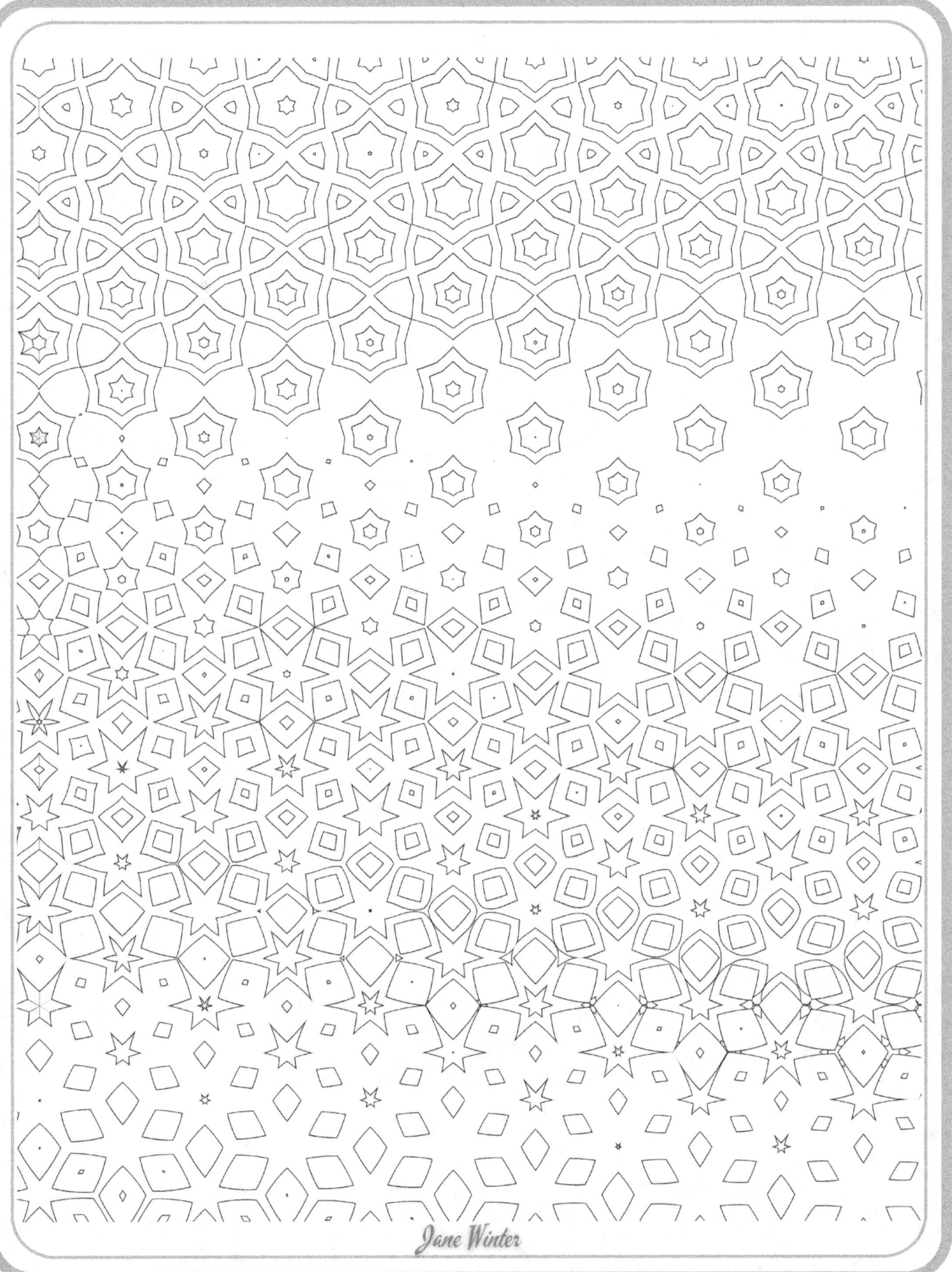

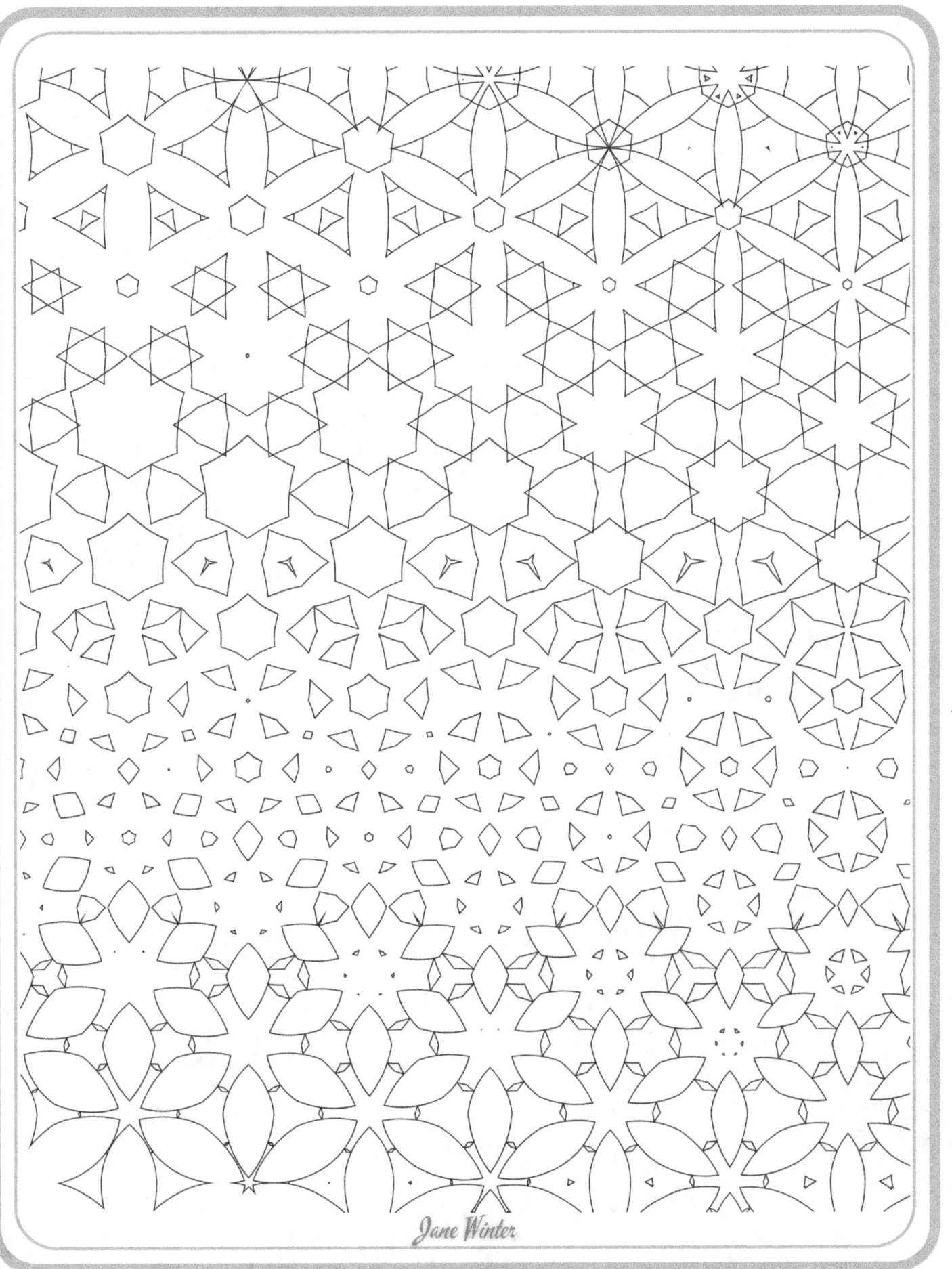

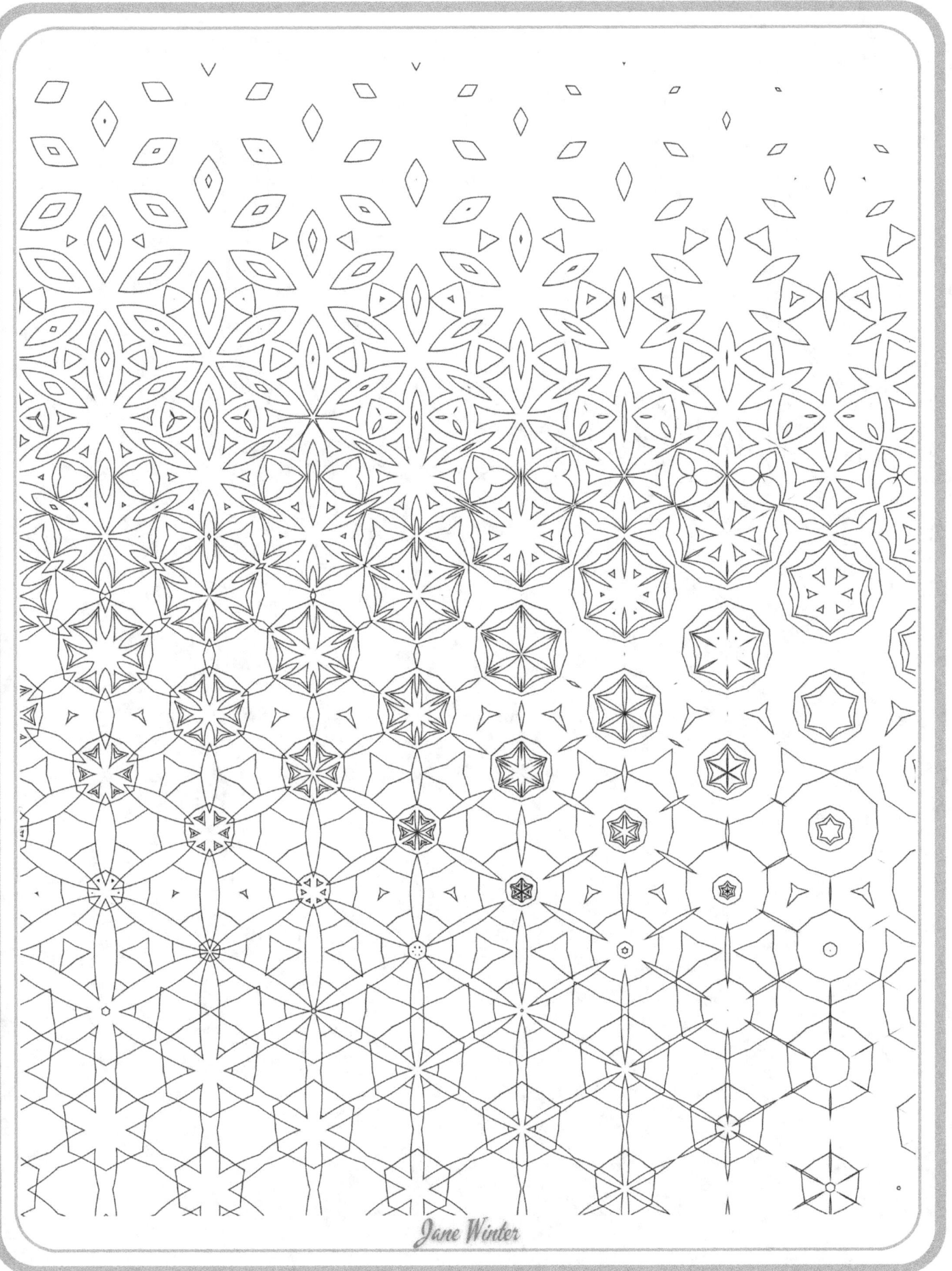

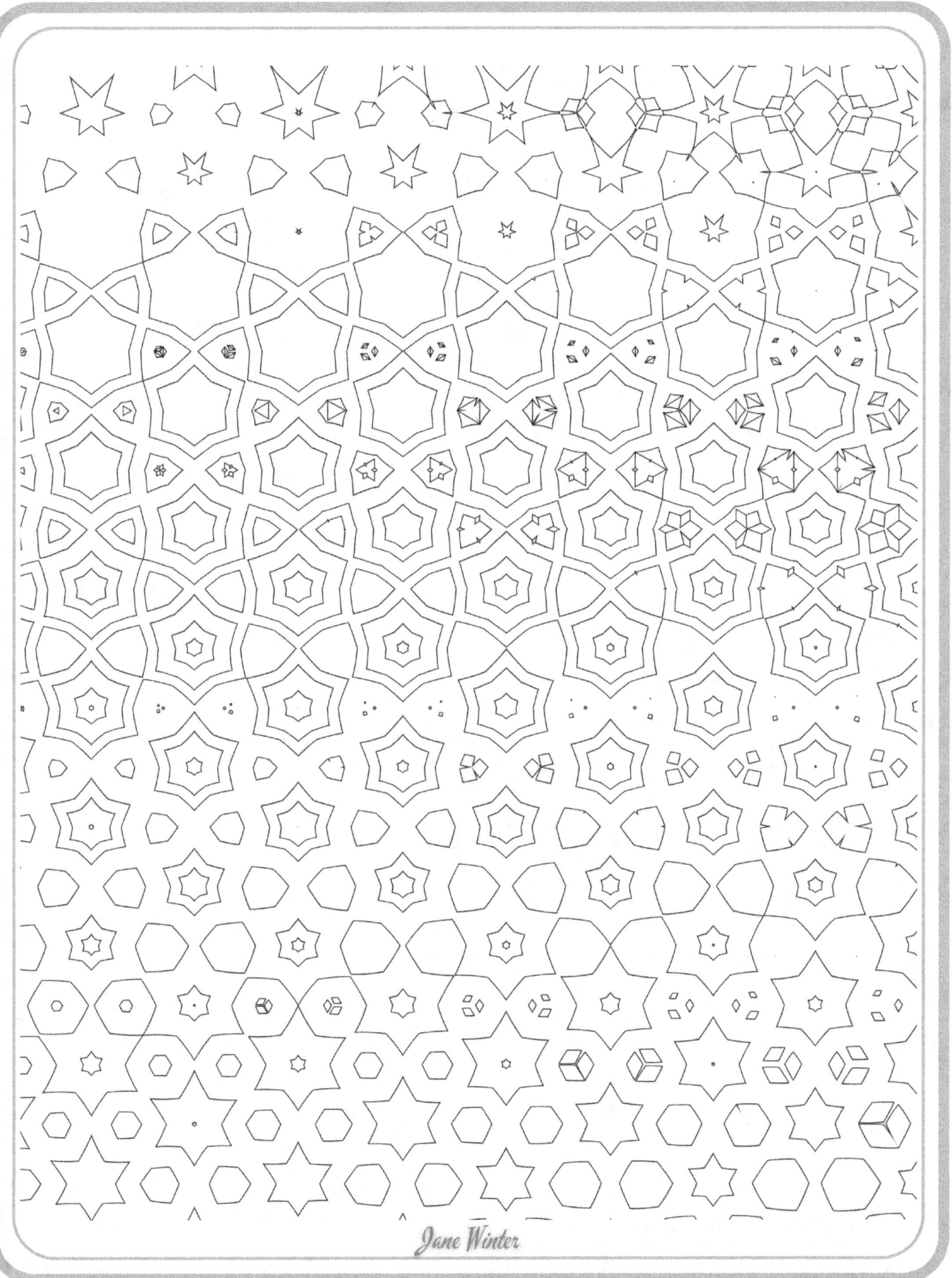

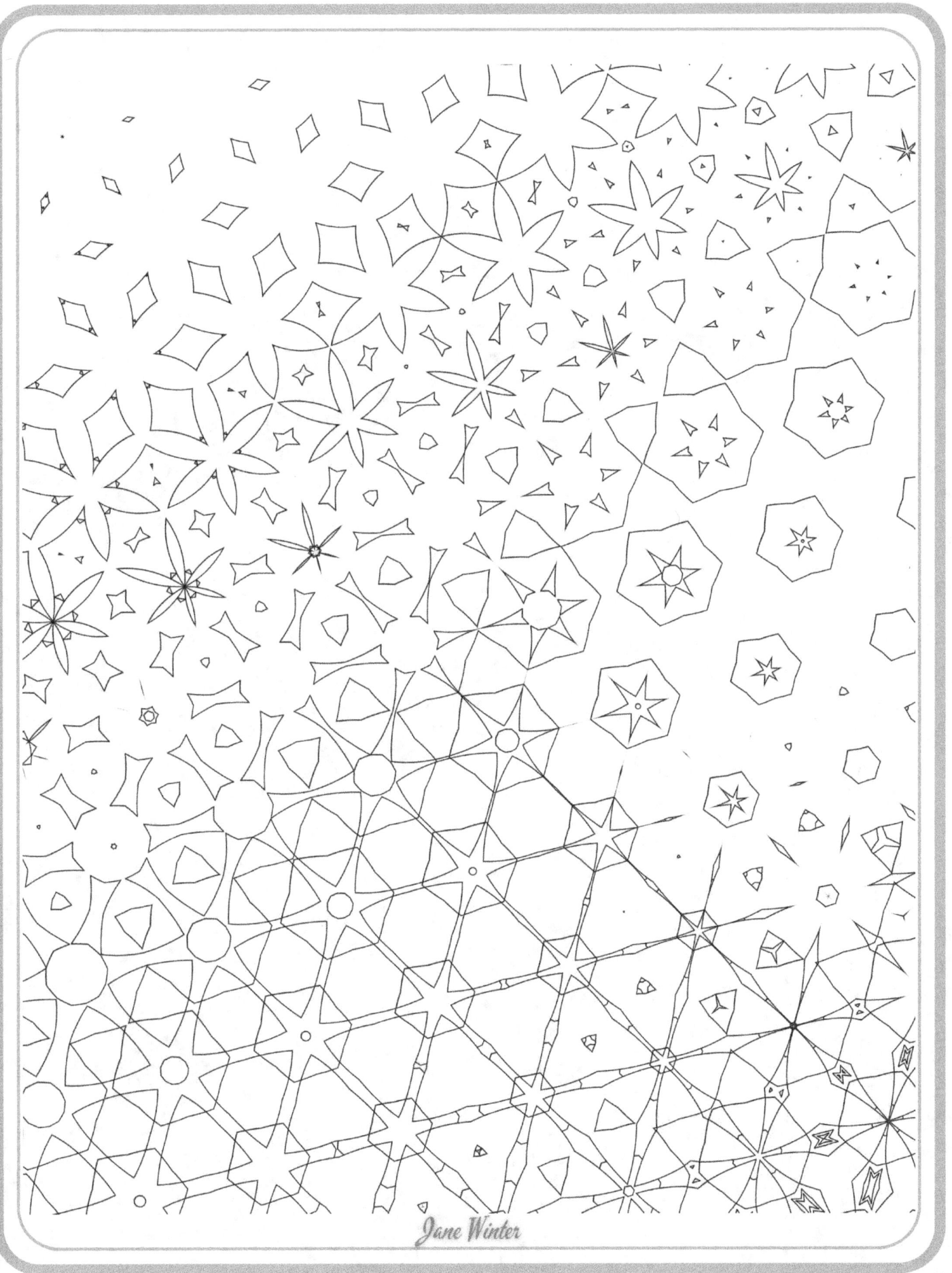

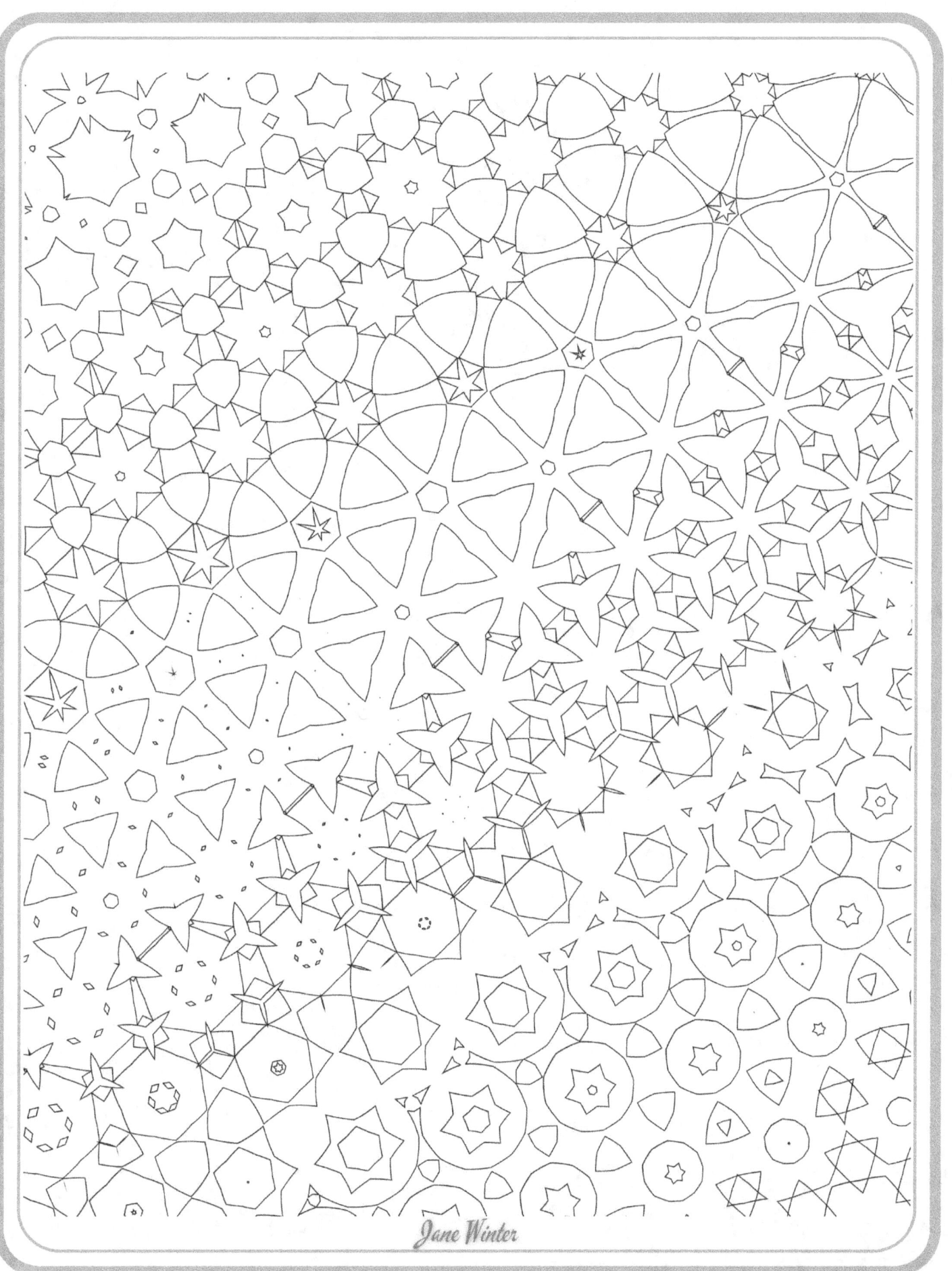

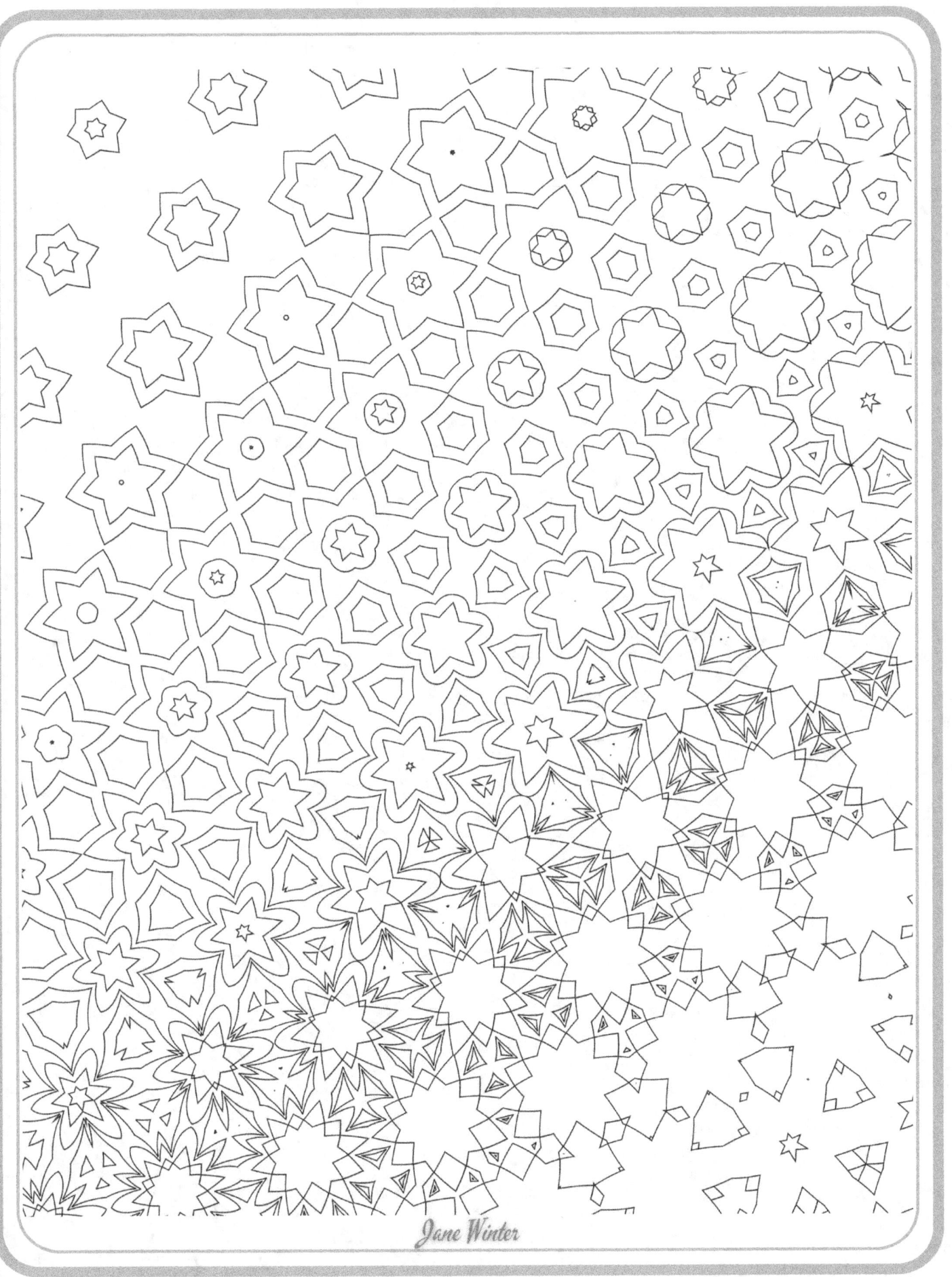

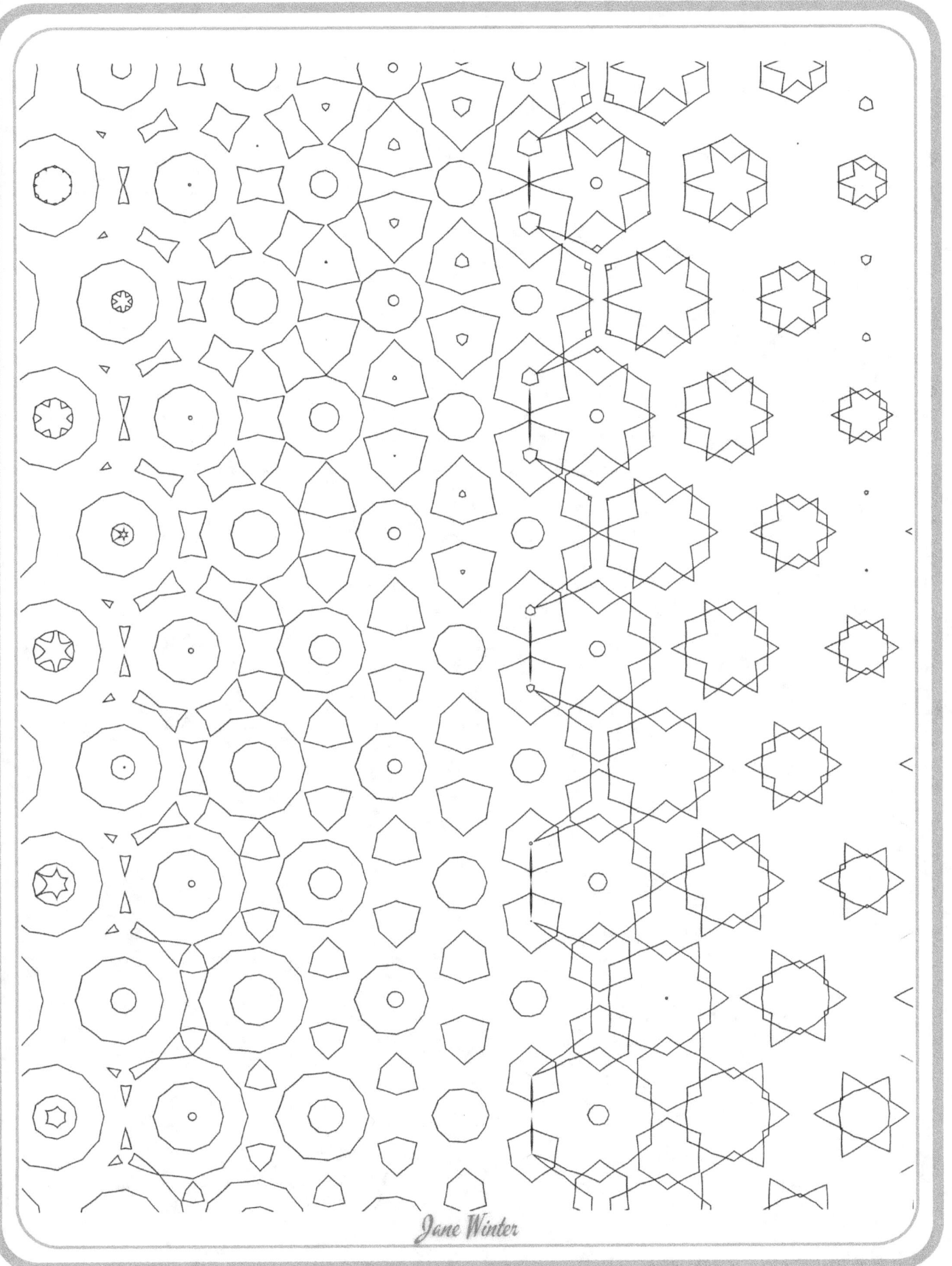

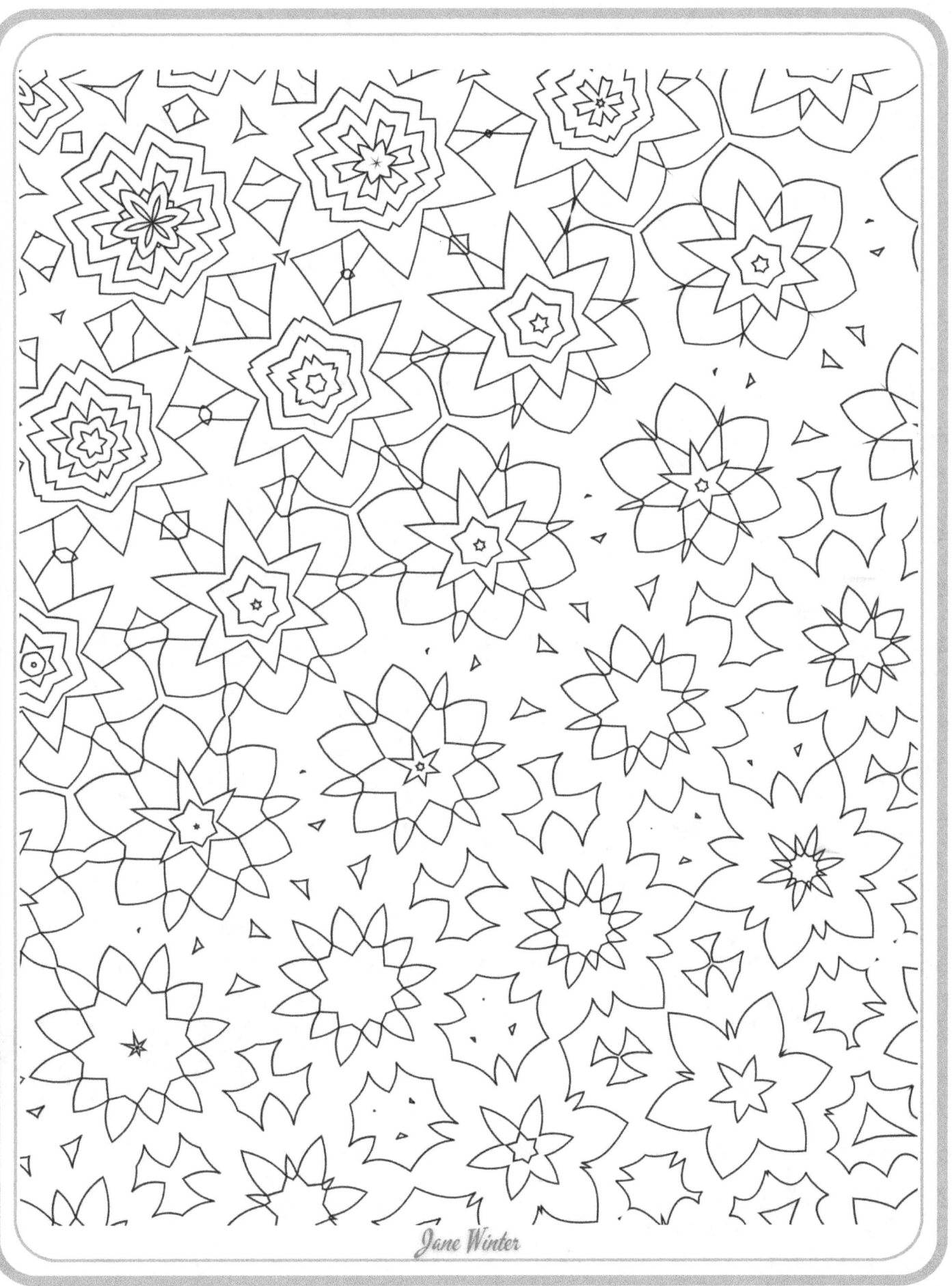

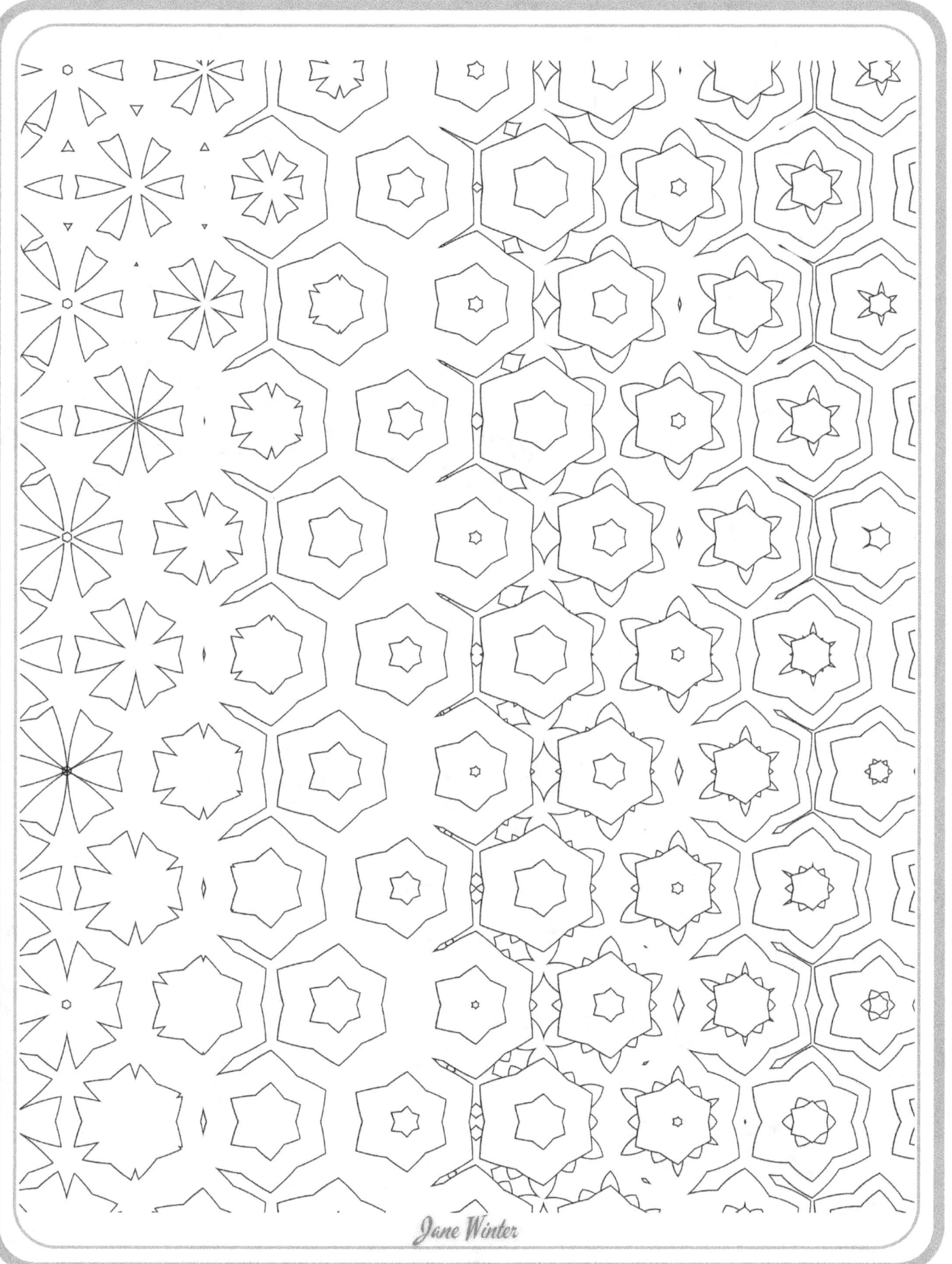

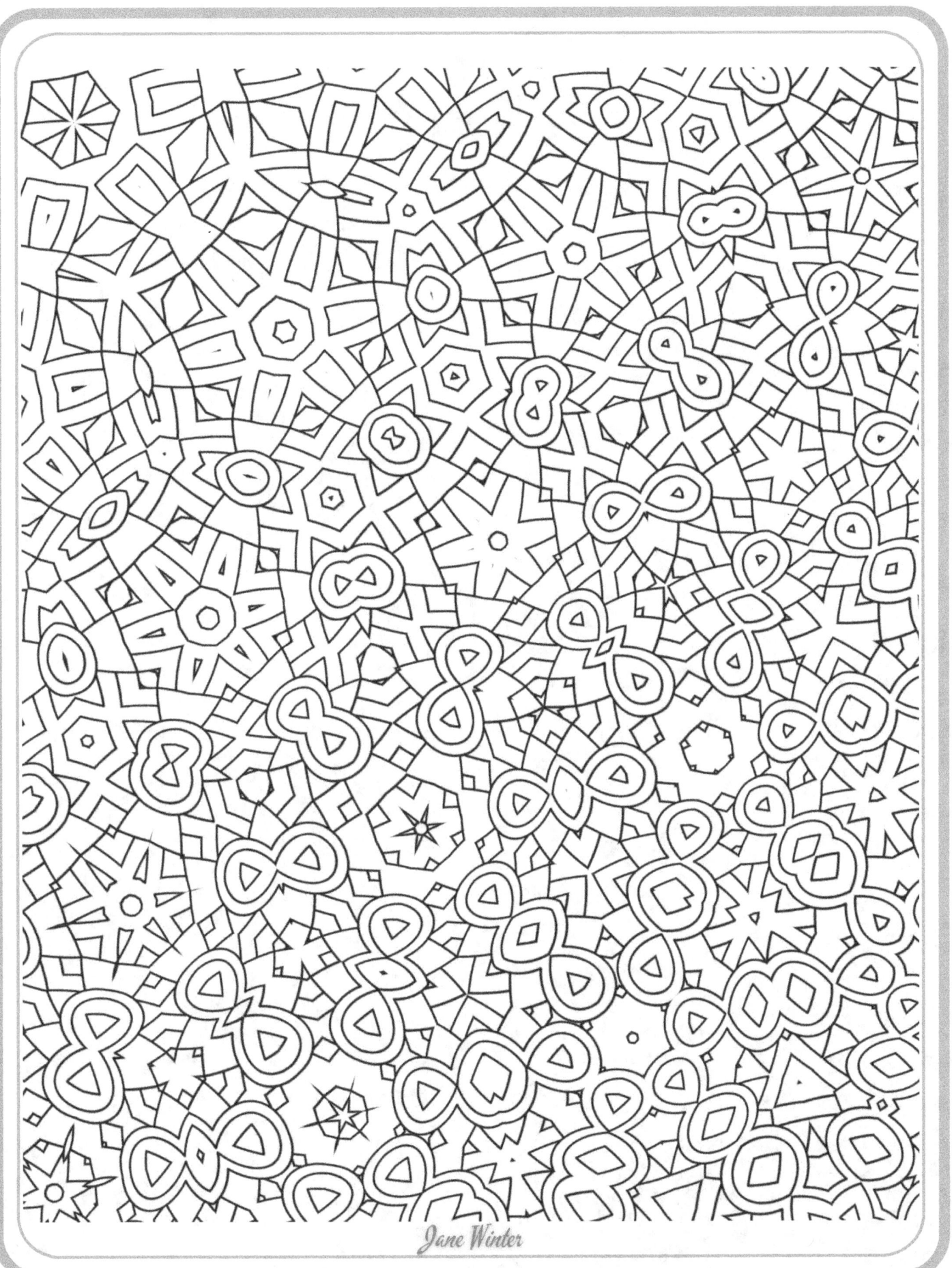
Jane Winter

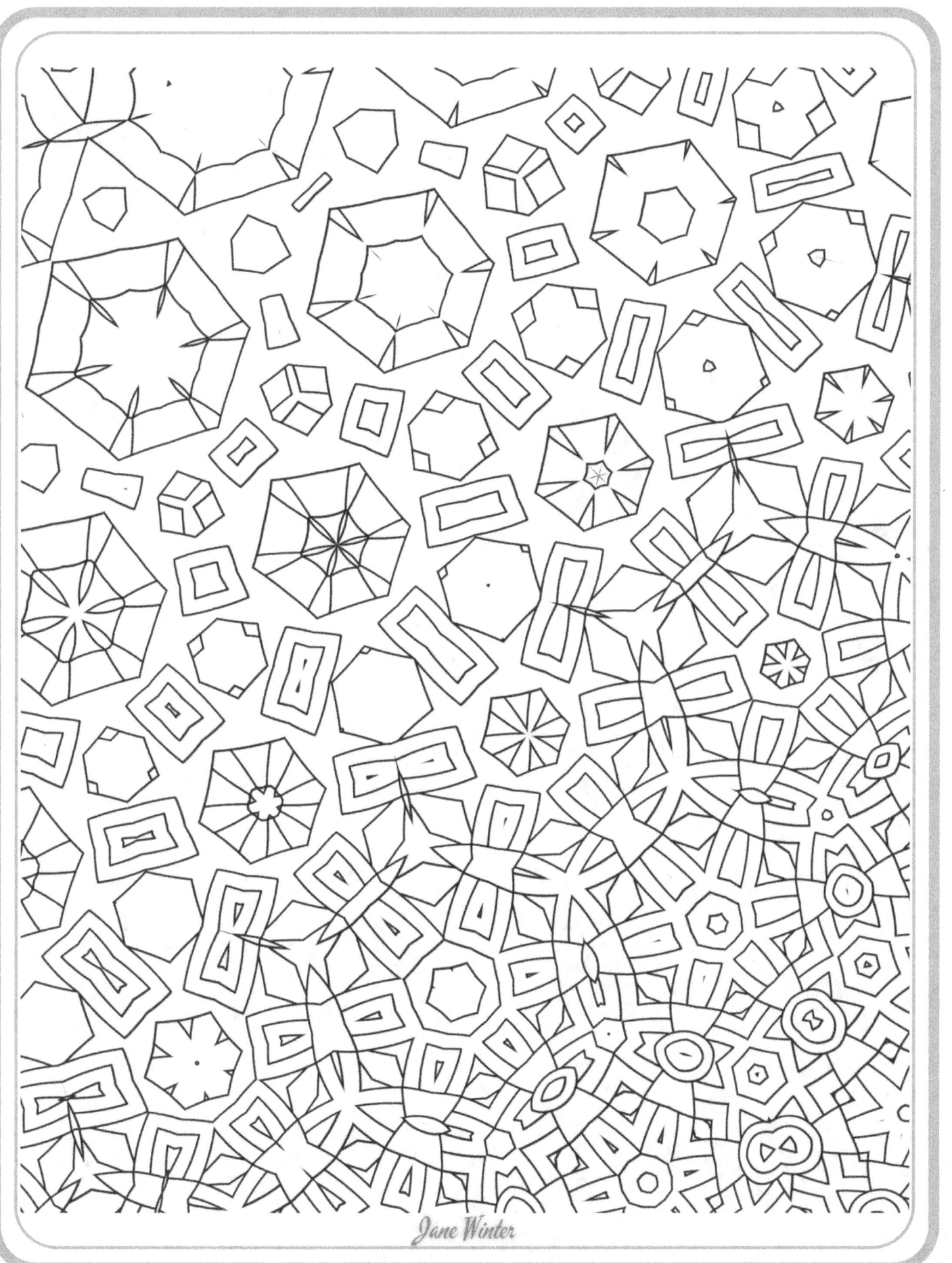

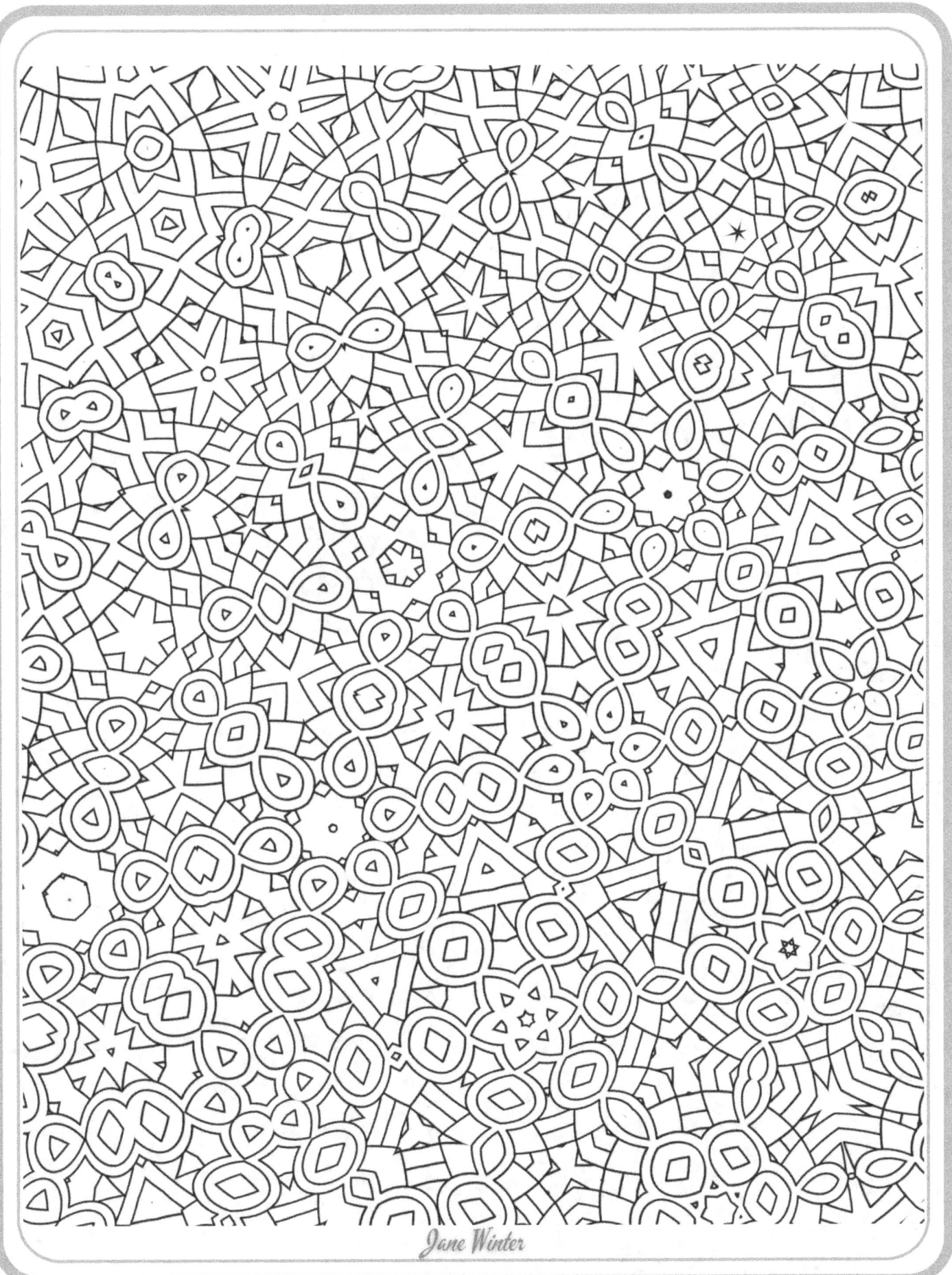

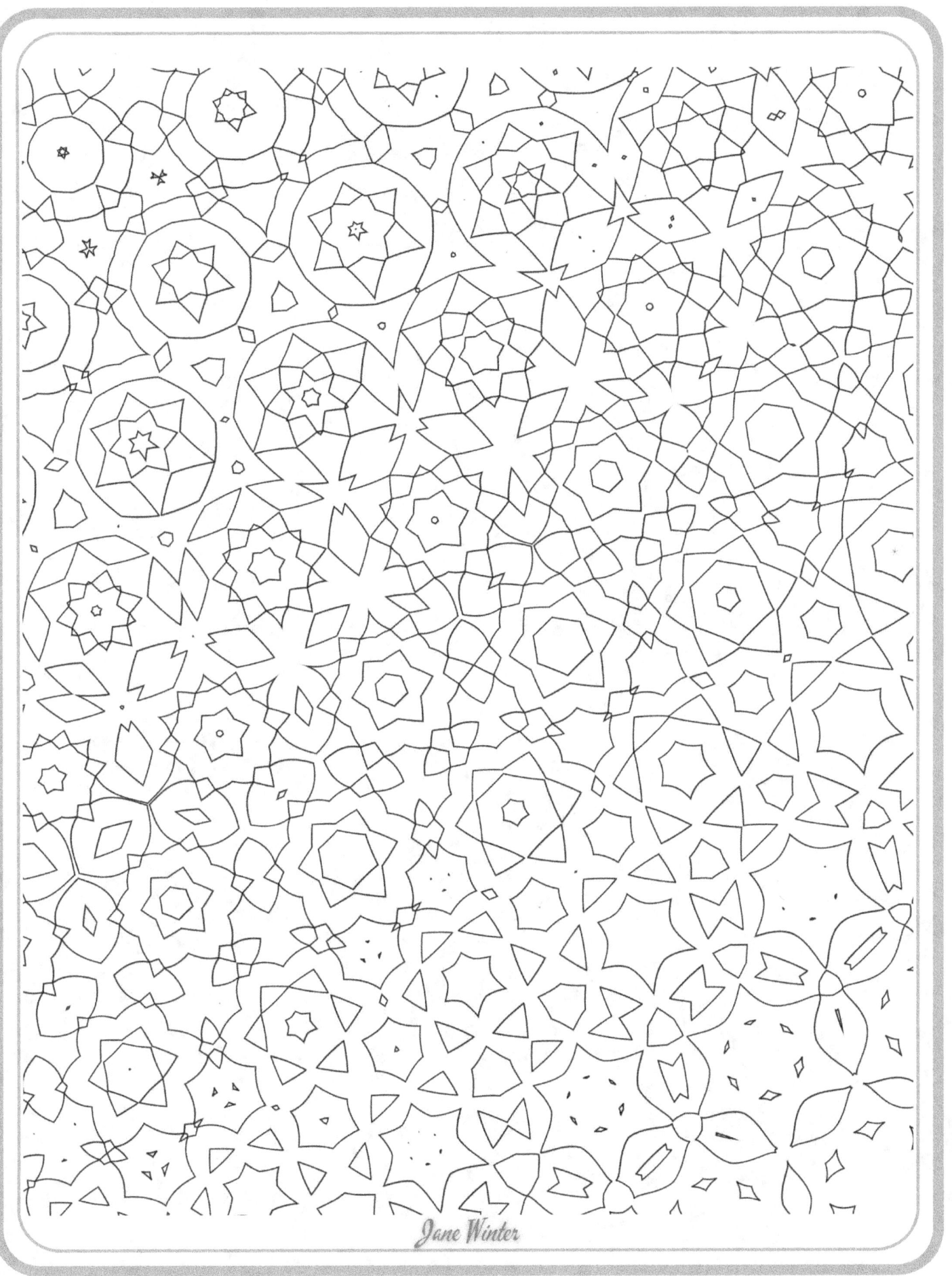

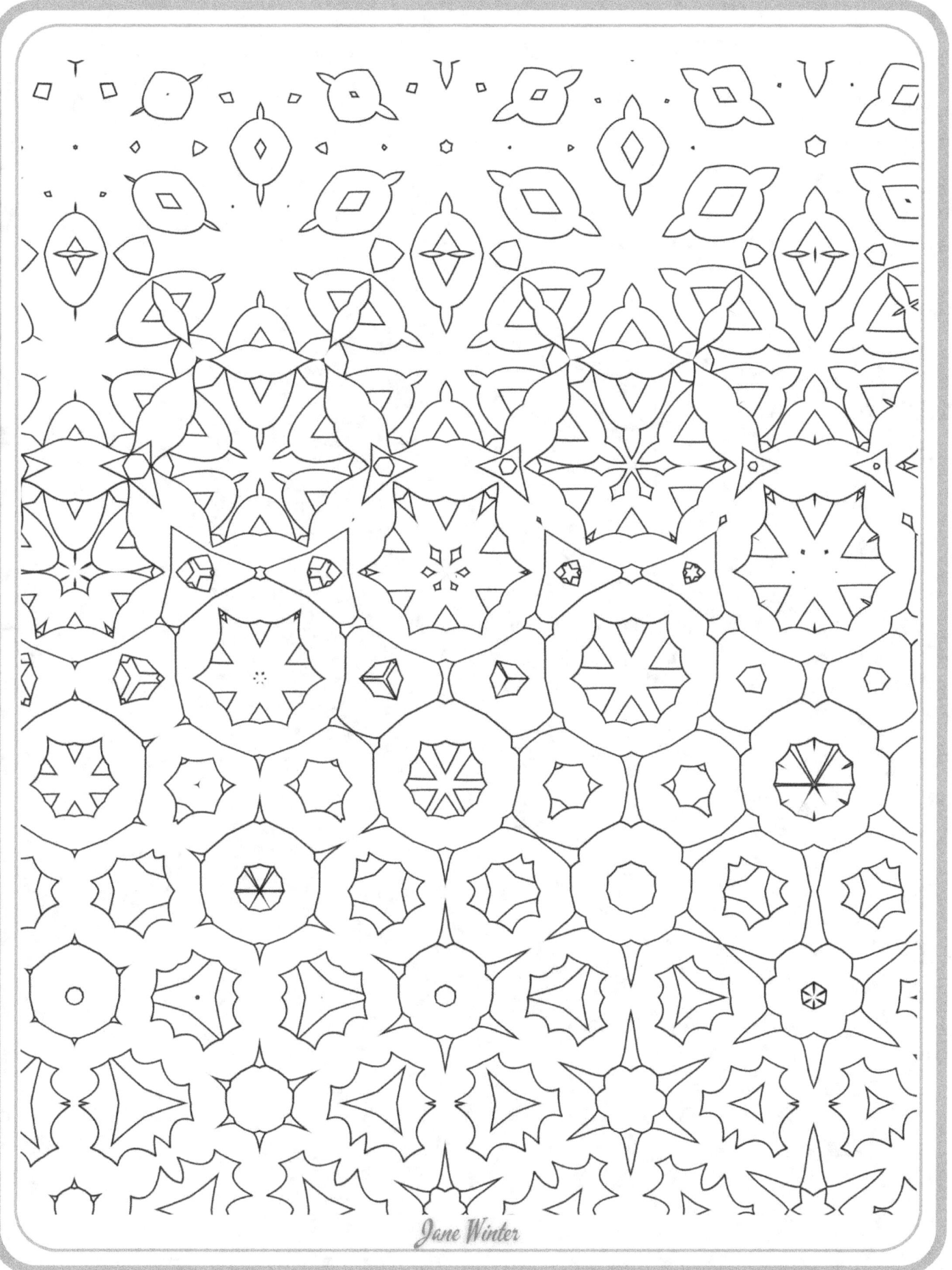

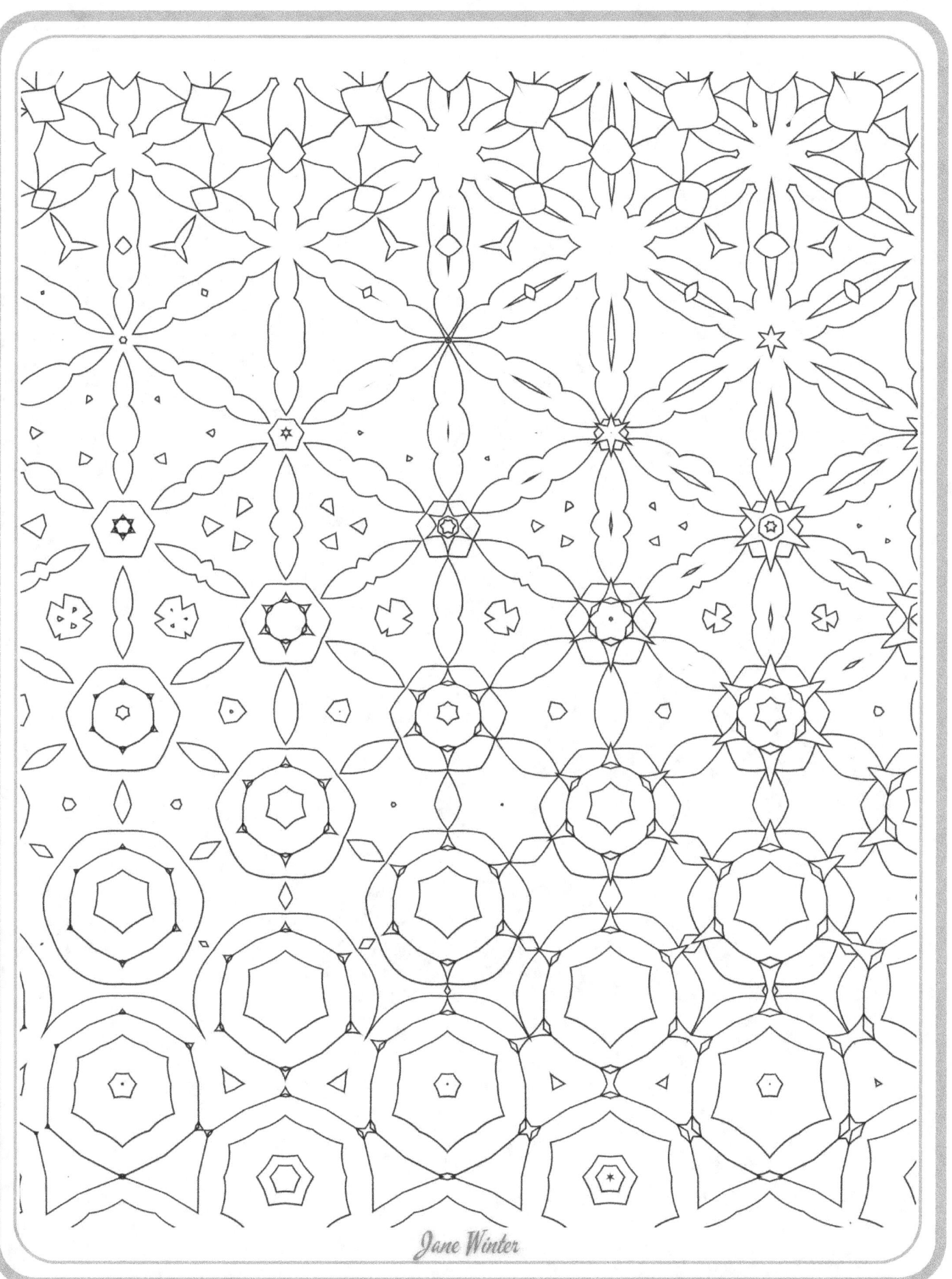

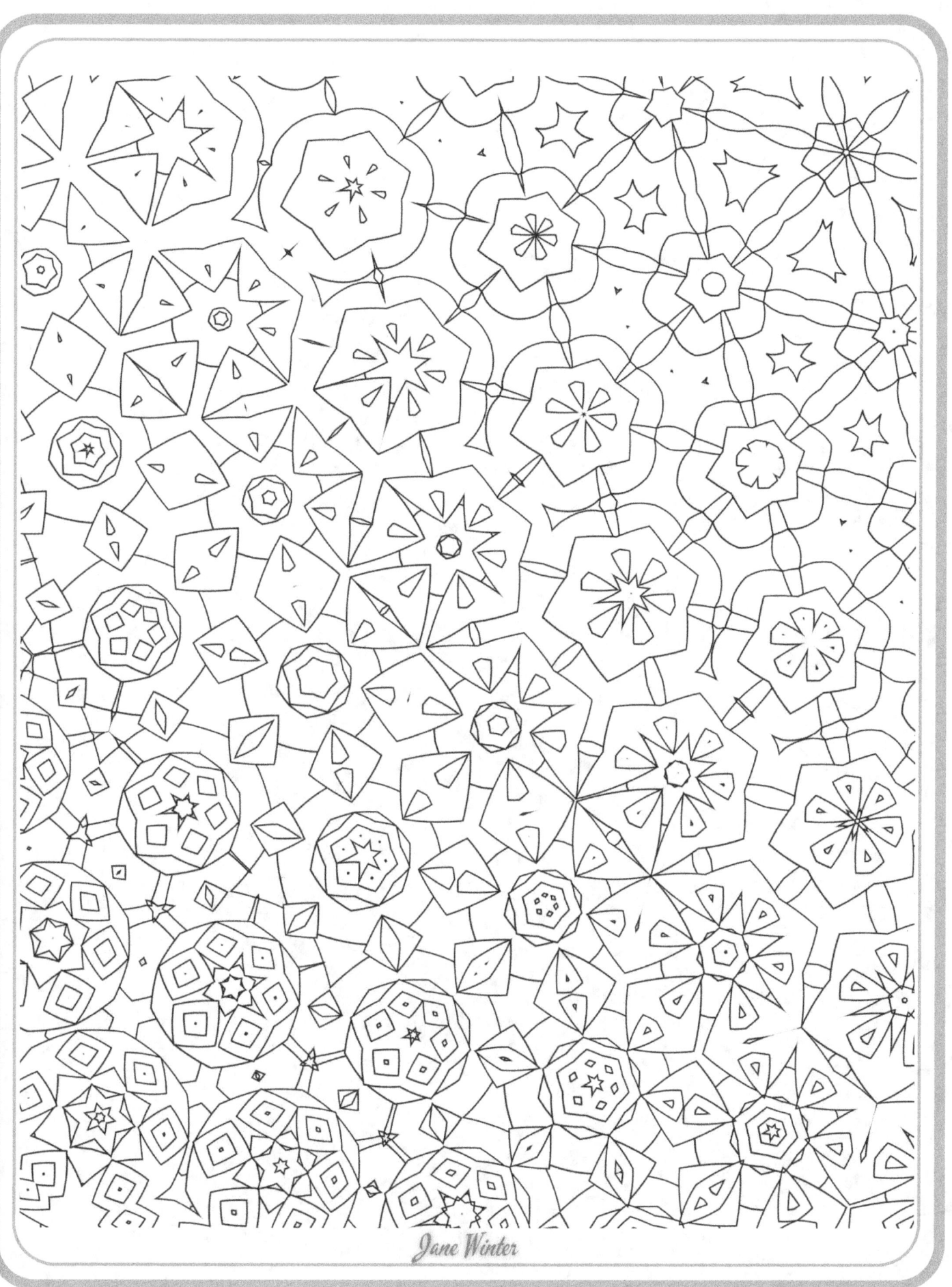

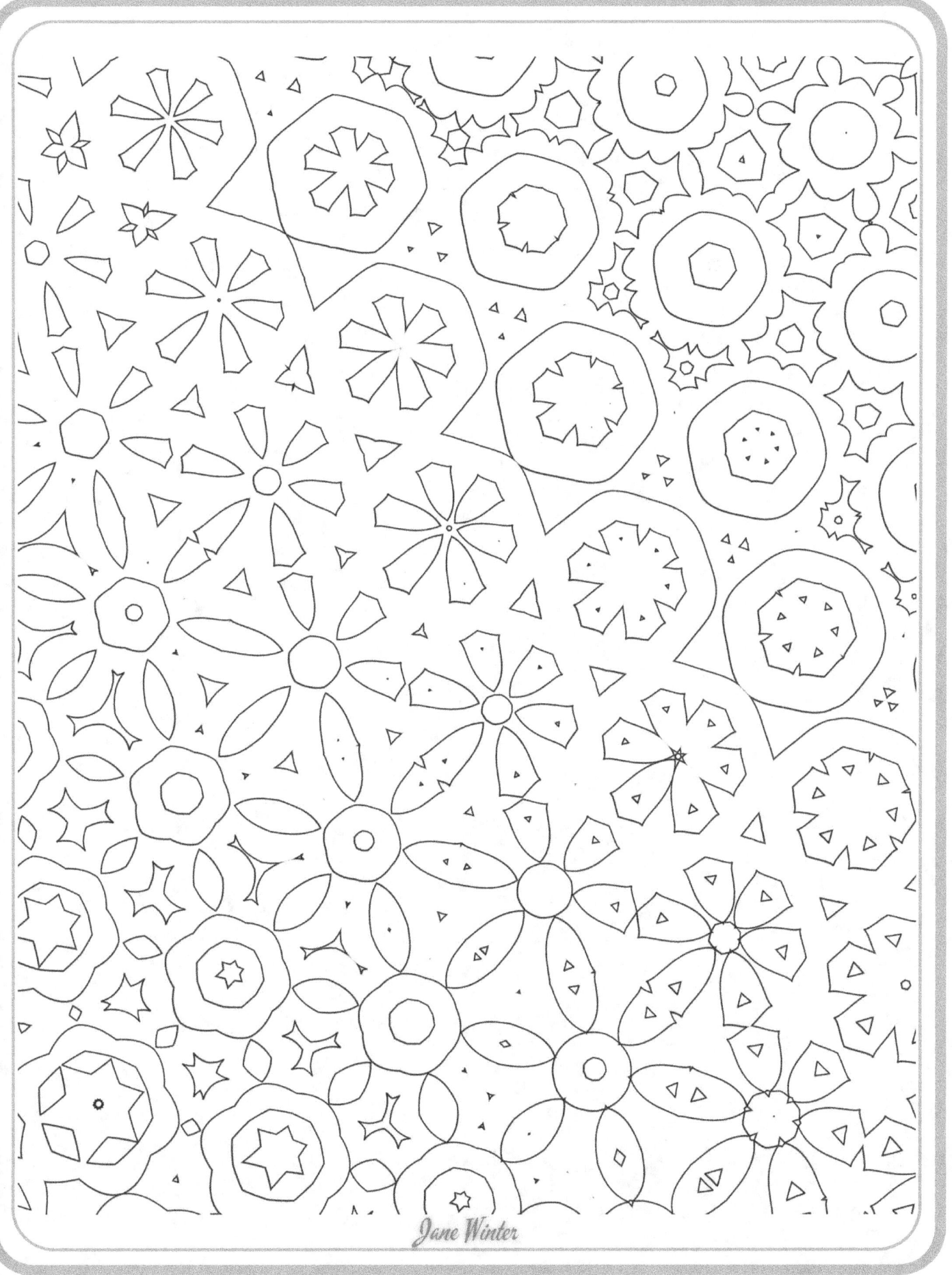

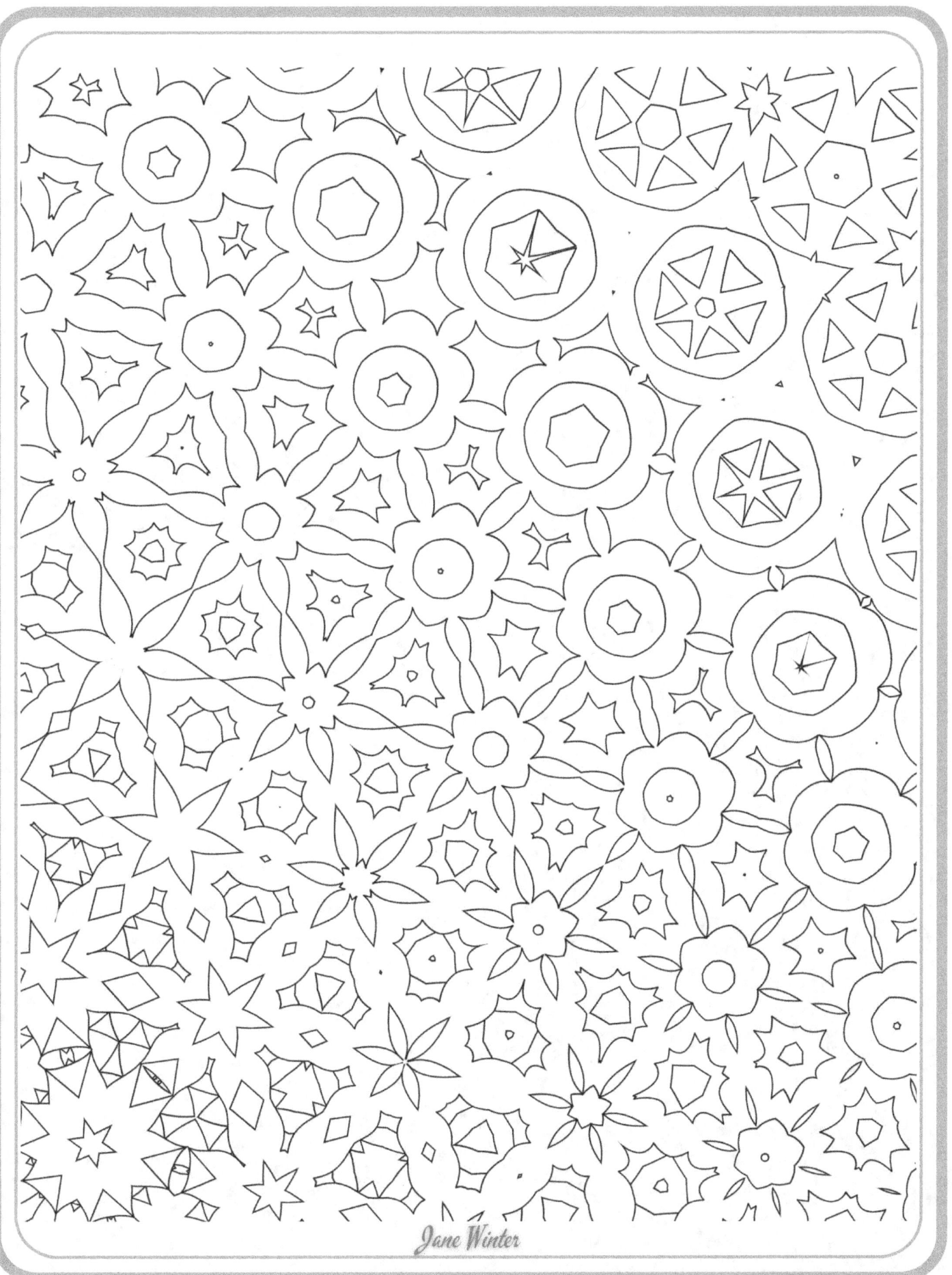
Jane Winter

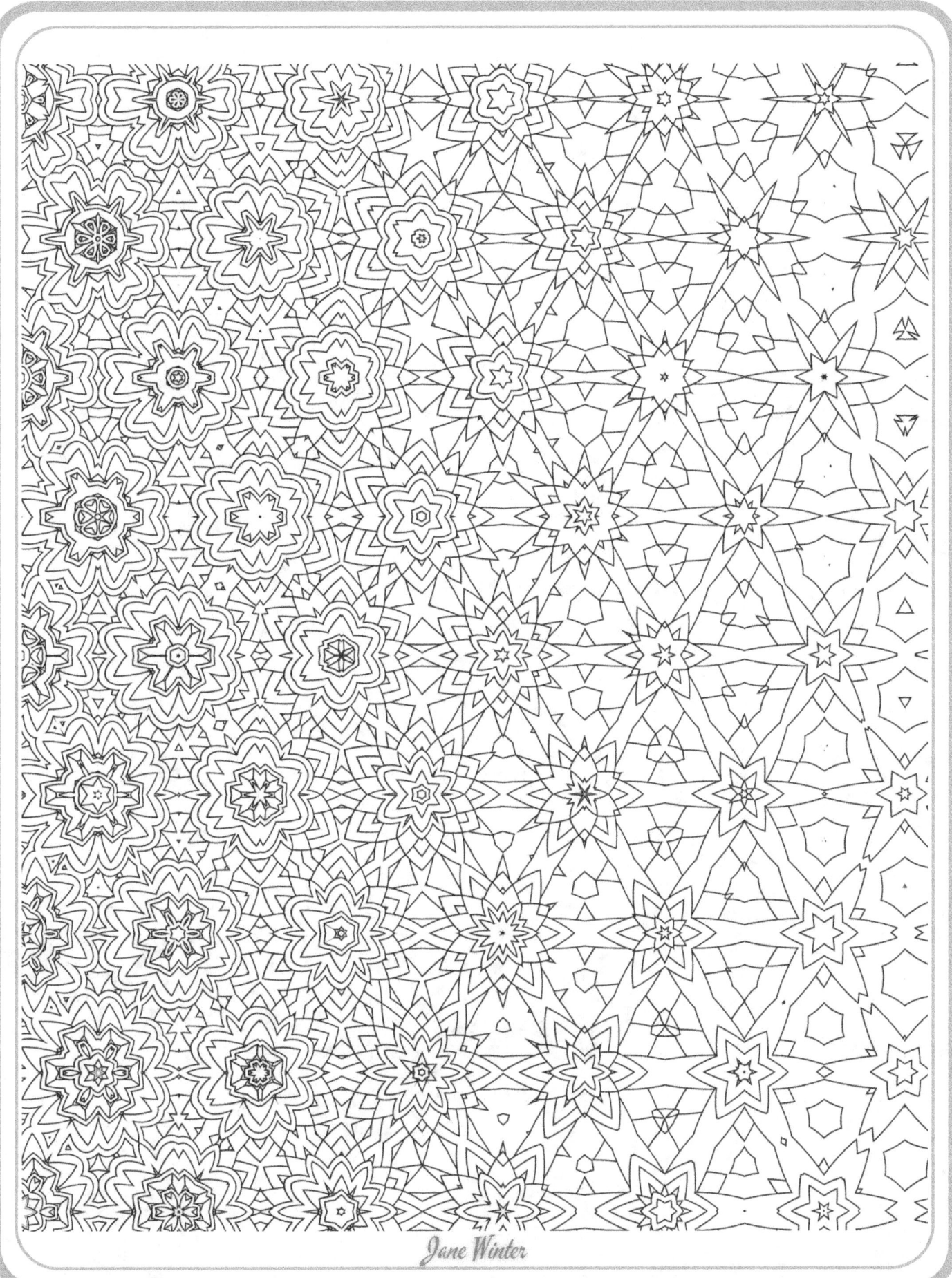
Jane Winter

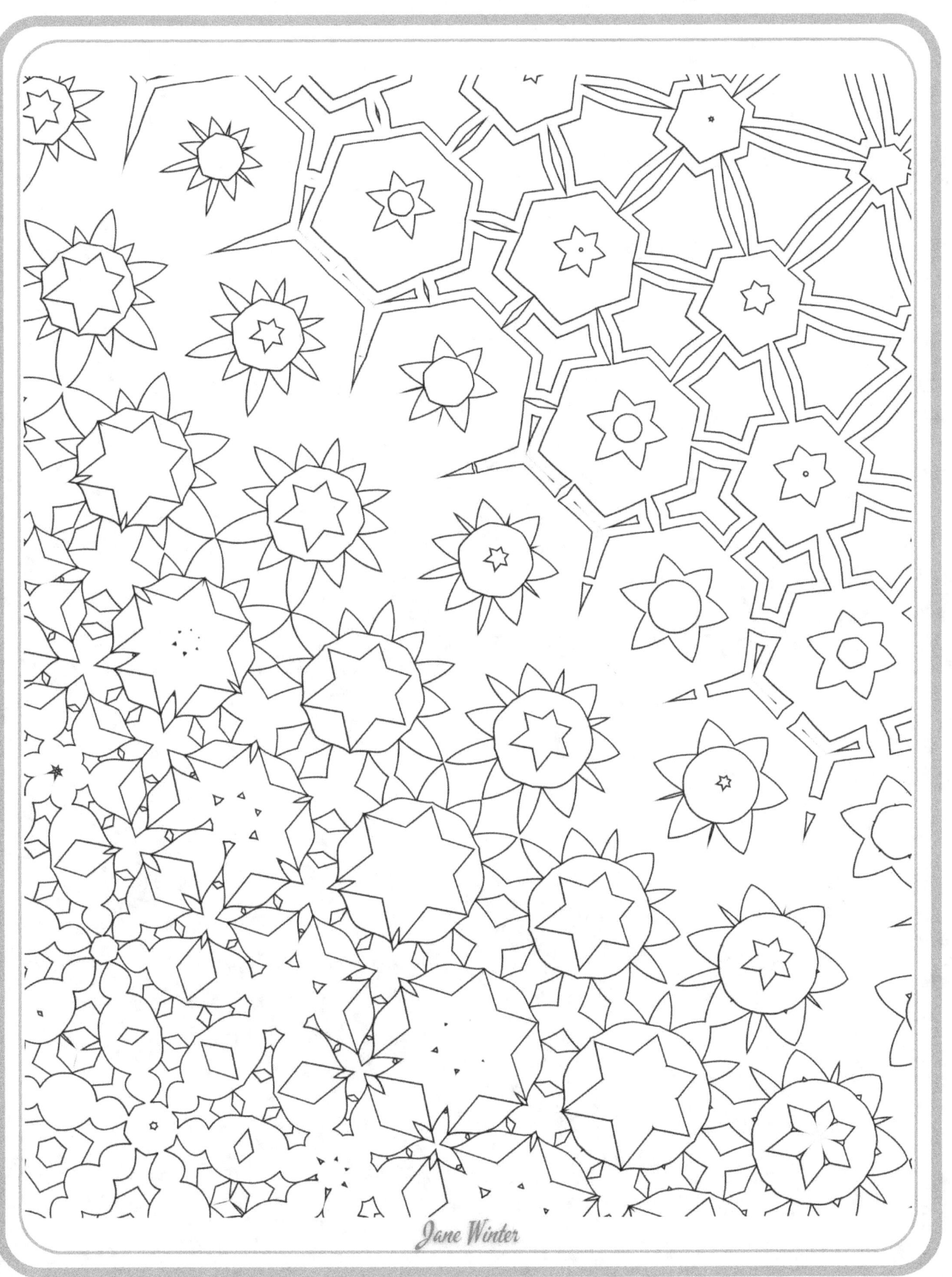

Jane Winter

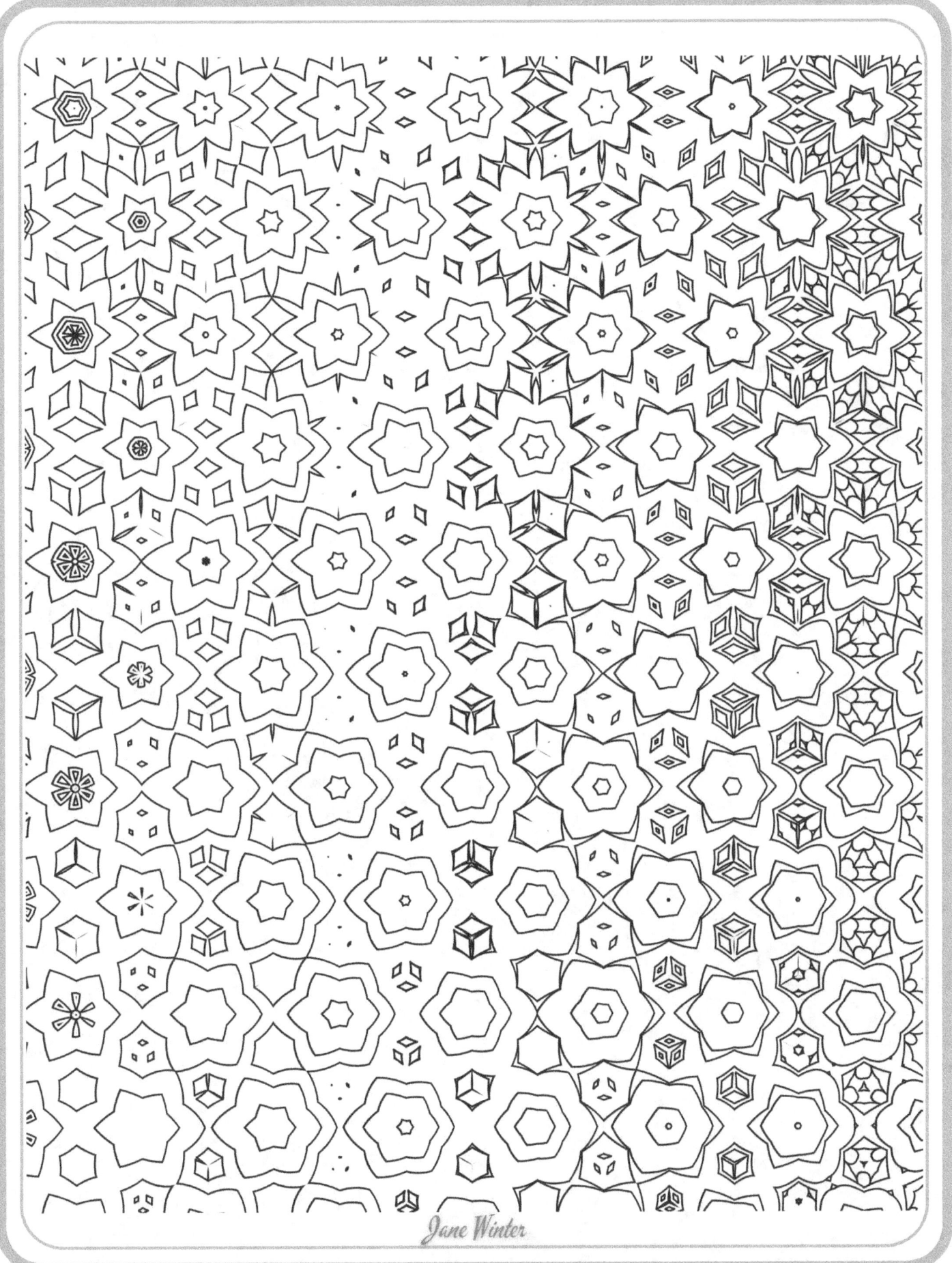

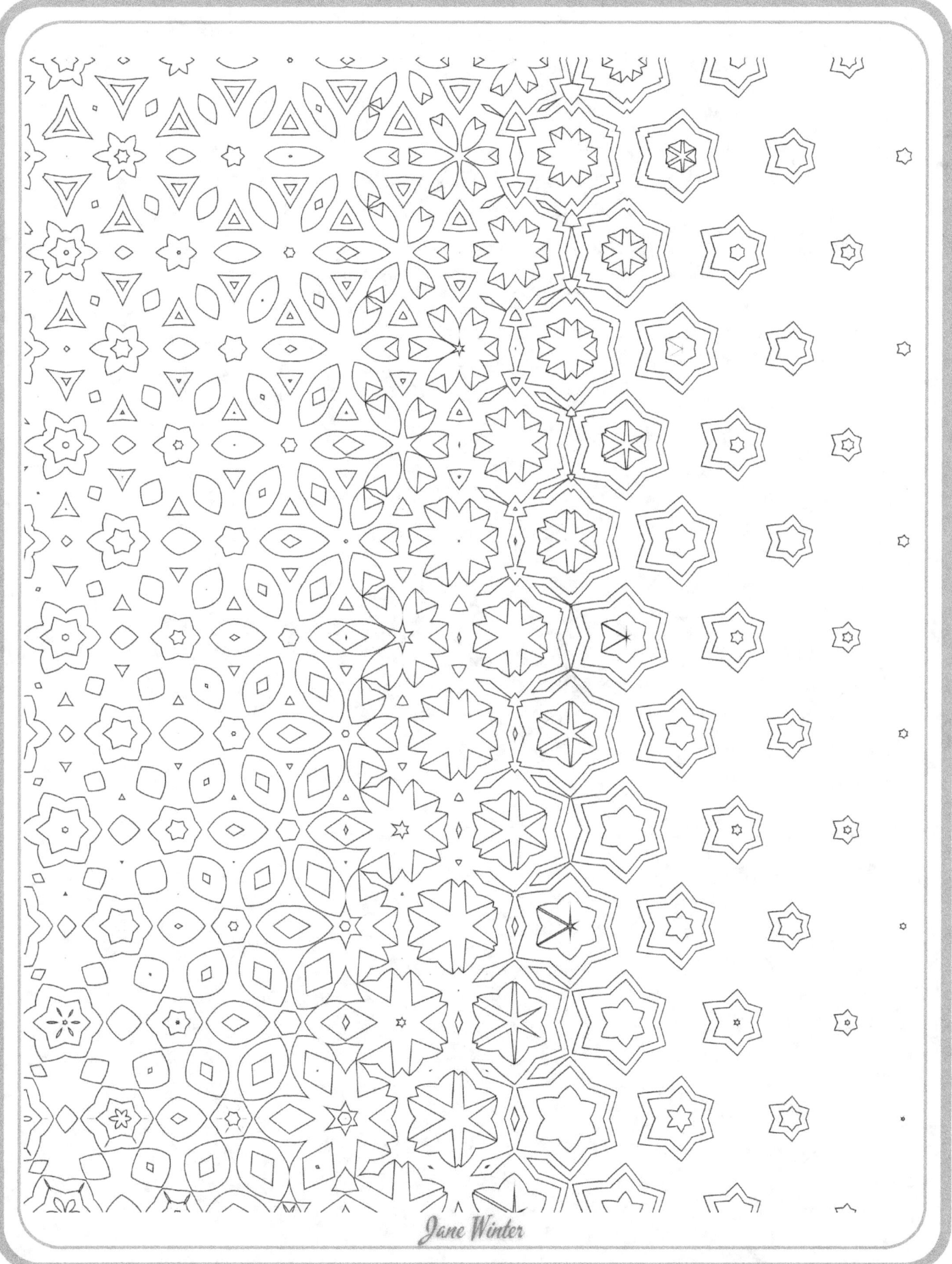

Jane Winter

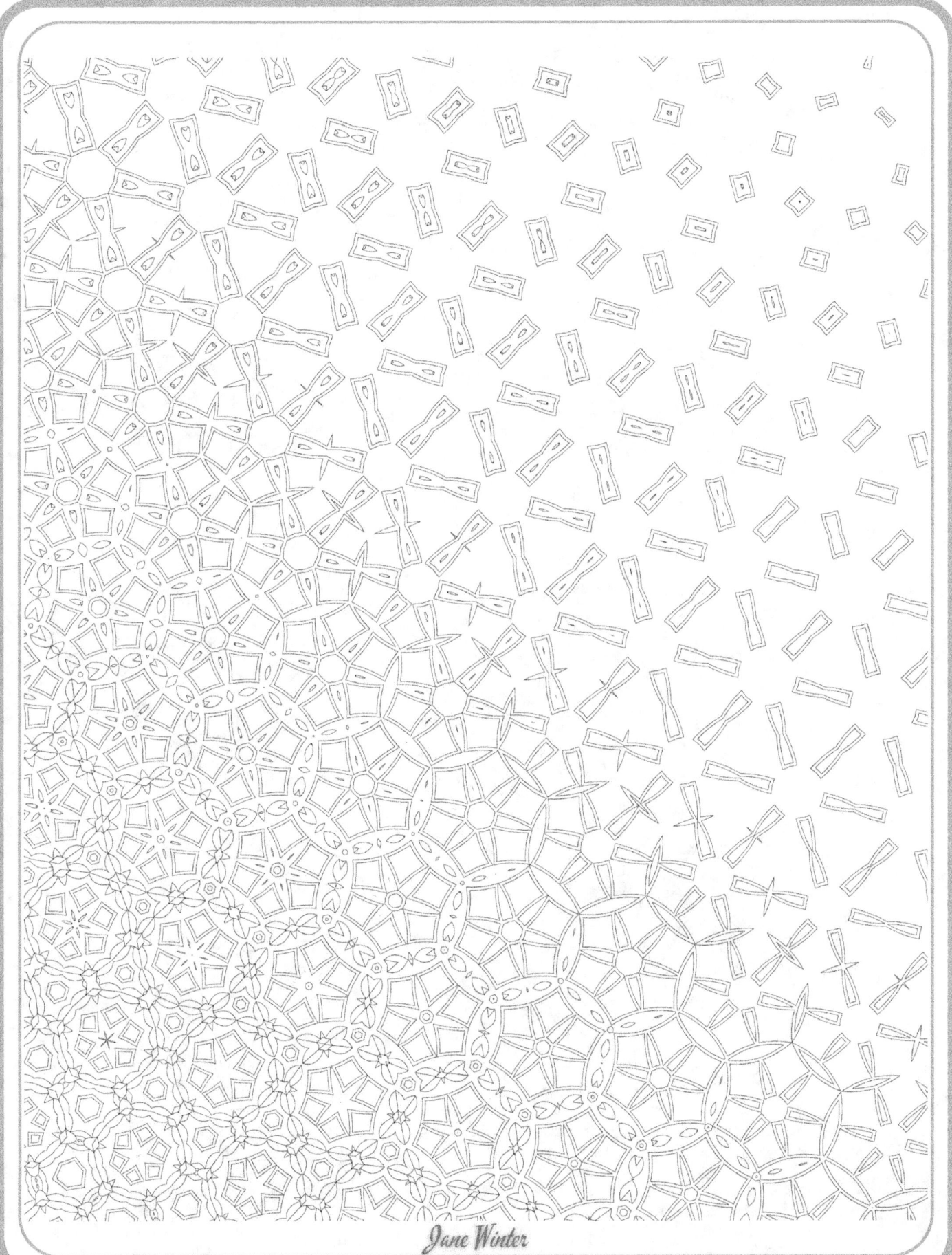

Jane Winter

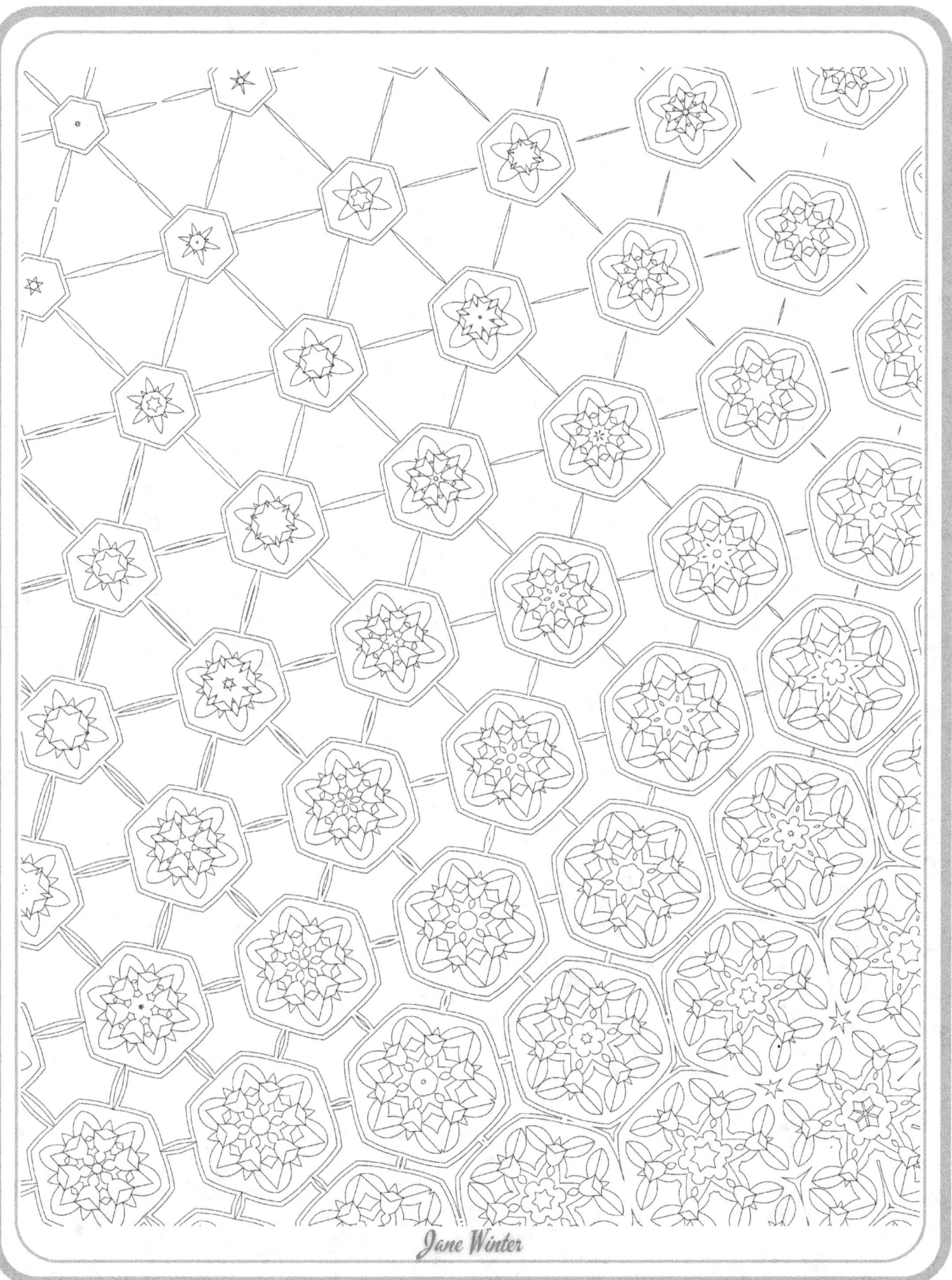

Jane Winter

Bonus Page
More in: "Love Mandalas Coloring Book"

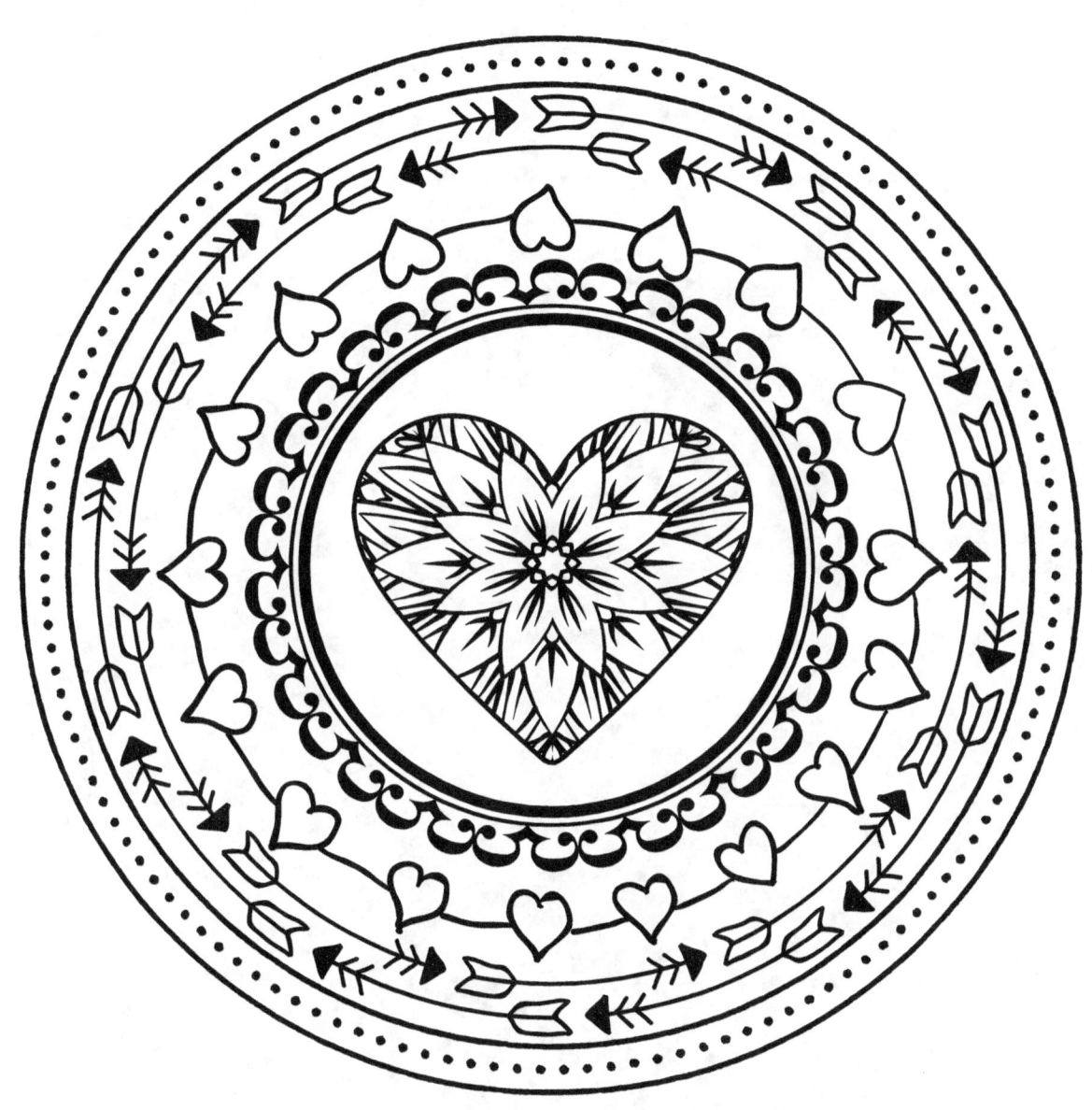

Jane Winter

Jane Winter

Bonus Page
More in: "Christmas Gnomes Coloring Book"

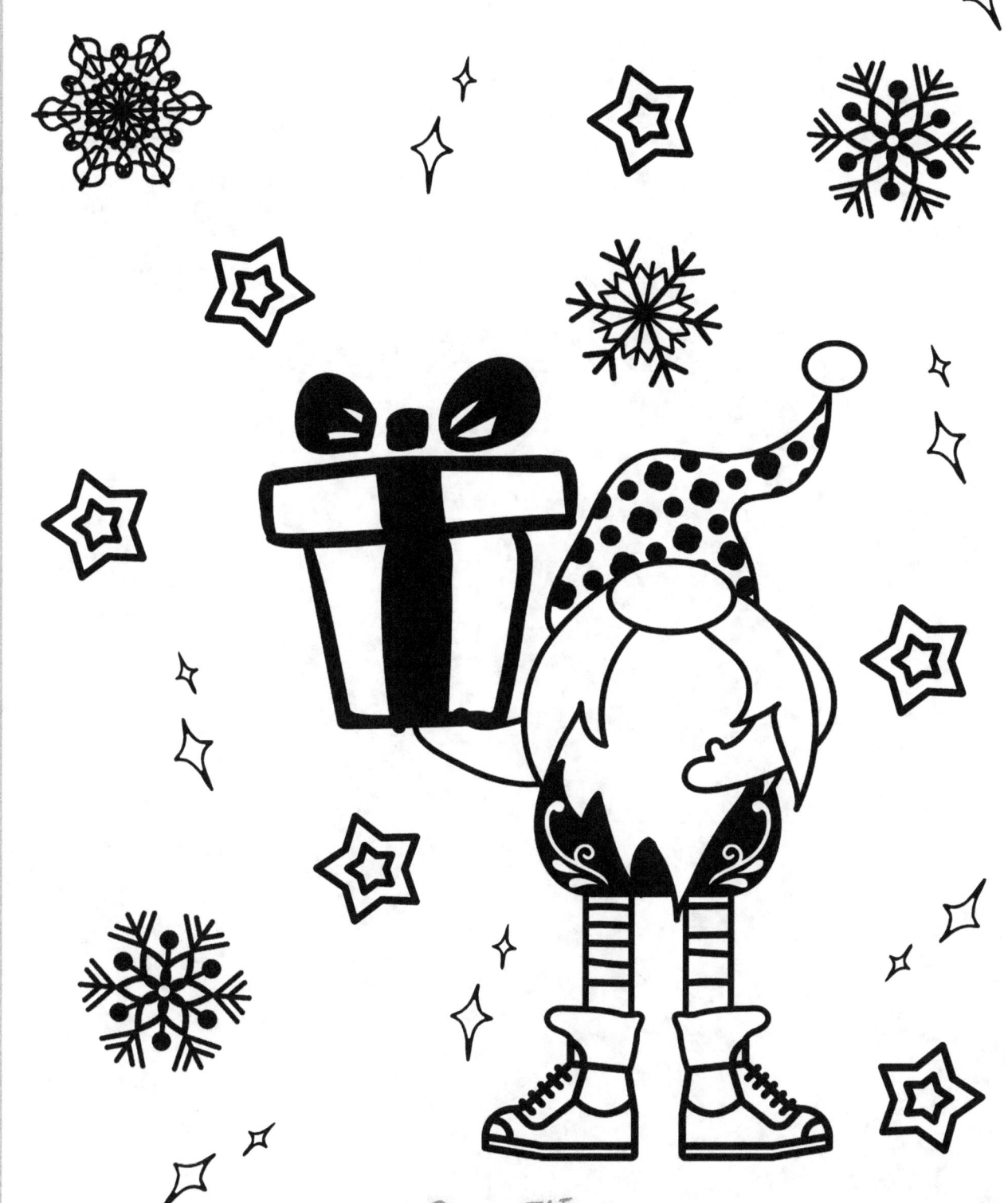

Jane Winter

Bonus Page
More in: "Large Print Geometric Coloring Book - Vol.1"

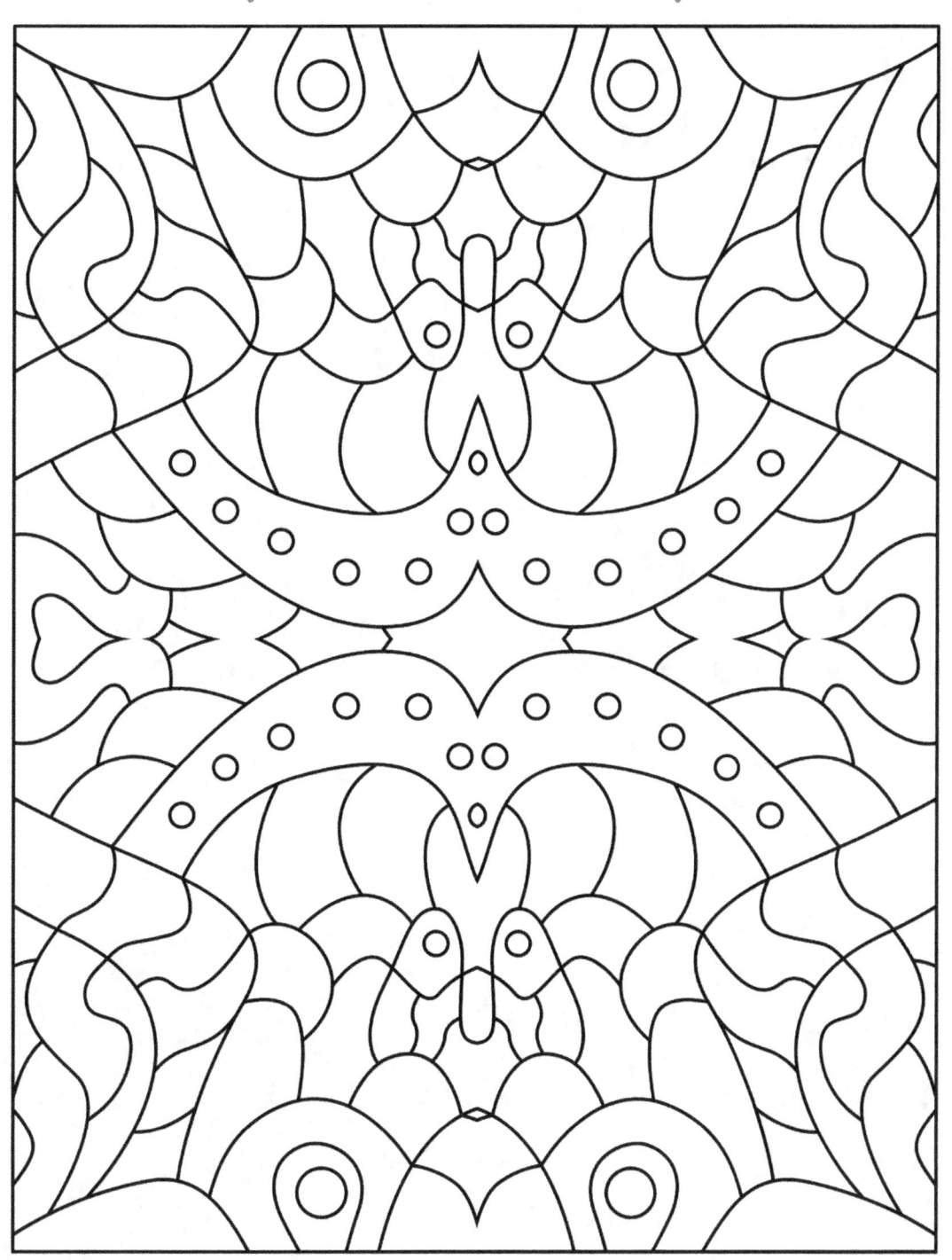

Jane Winter

Bonus Page
More in: "Christmas Coloring Book for Adults"

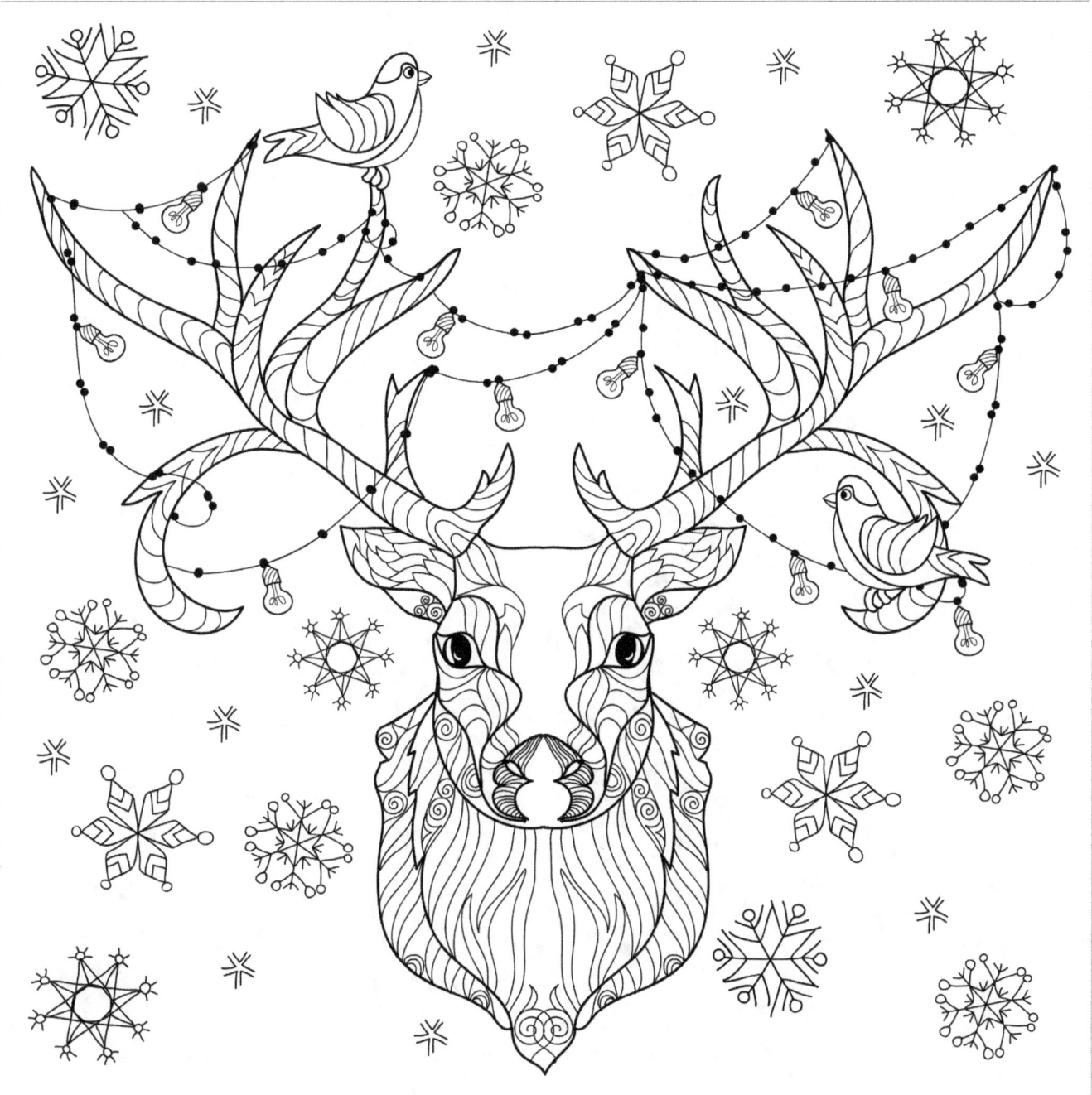

Jane Winter

Easy Mandalas Coloring Book for Adults

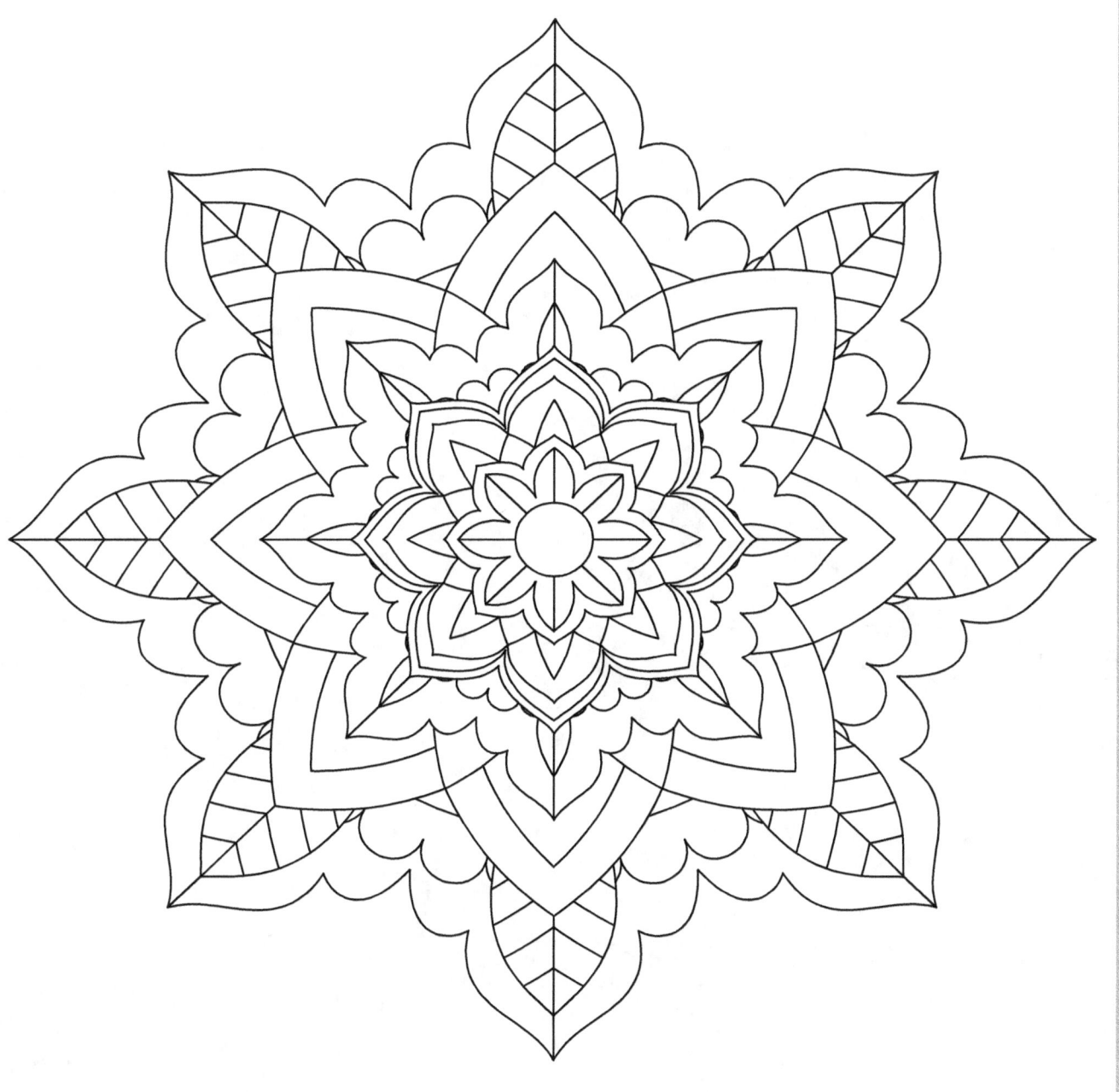

Jane Winter

Jane Winter

Thank you so much for purchasing my book!

If you enjoyed this book, please leave a review on Amazon!

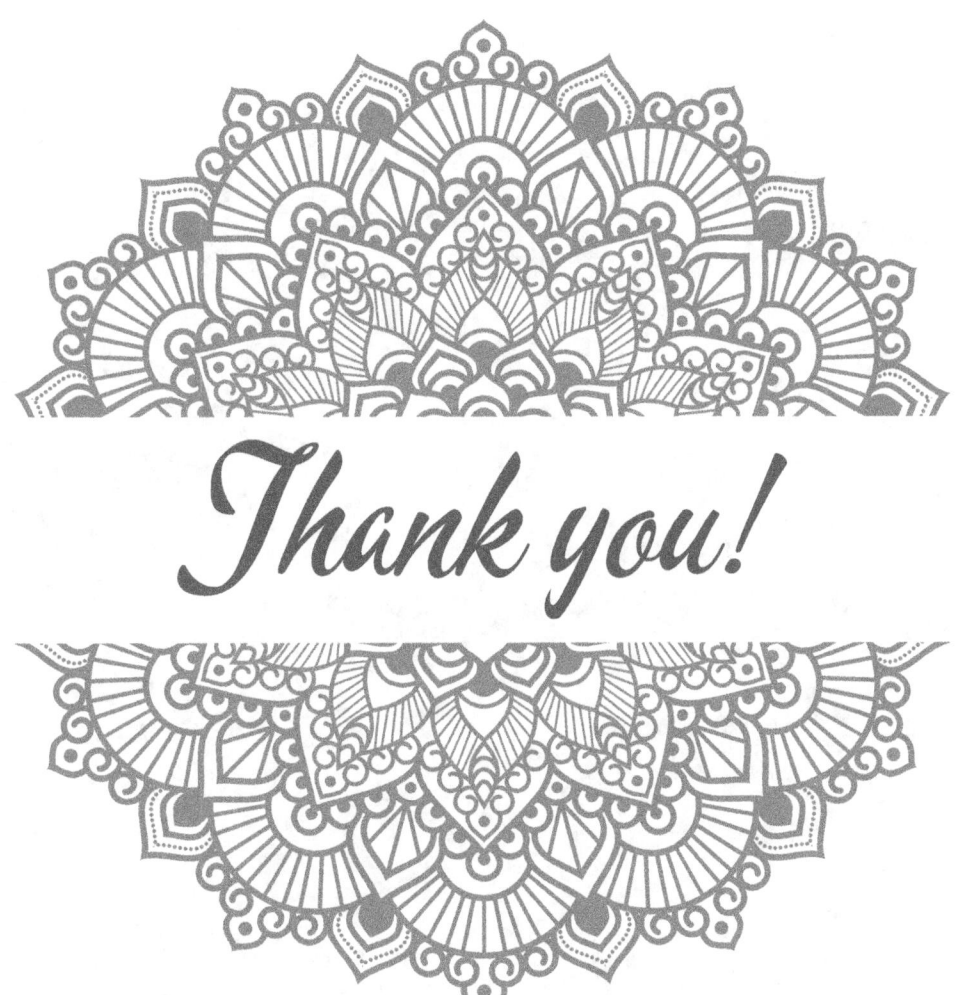

Jane Winter

www.ingramcontent.com/pod-product-compliance
Lightning Source LLC
Chambersburg PA
CBHW080552220526
45466CB00010B/3123